MW01415405

And the Dragons
Do Come

And the Dragons Do Come

Raising a Transgender Kid in Rural America

Sim Butler

THE NEW PRESS
NEW YORK
LONDON

© 2025 by Sim Butler
All rights reserved.
No part of this book may be reproduced, in any form, without written permission from the publisher.

Requests for permission to reproduce selections from this book should be made through our website: https://thenewpress.org/contact-us.

Published in the United States by The New Press, New York, 2025

Distributed by Two Rivers Distribution

ISBN 978-1-62097-904-4 (hc)
ISBN 978-1-62097-994-5 (ebook)

CIP data is available

The New Press publishes books that promote and enrich public discussion and understanding of the issues vital to our democracy and to a more equitable world. These books are made possible by the enthusiasm of our readers; the support of a committed group of donors, large and small; the collaboration of our many partners in the independent media and the not-for-profit sector; booksellers, who often hand-sell New Press books; librarians; and above all by our authors.

www.thenewpress.org

Composition by Dix Digital Prepress and Design

This book was set in Garamond Premier Pro

Printed in the United States of America

10 9 8 7 6 5 4 3 2

To my favorite daughter, whichever of you it is today

Contents

1. The Dead Named — 1
2. Memorabilia — 25
3. Playing Pretend — 61
4. Schooling — 83
5. Exercising Rights — 113
6. Seeking Health — 147
7. The Dragon — 163
8. Beyond Alabama — 179
9. Picking Our Ground — 201
   Epilogue — 221
   Acknowledgments — 225
   Appendix: For Readers' Reference — 227

I

The Dead Named

The first lesson I had in naming came at the dinner table. I was young, probably nine or ten, and we were living out in the country in Pike Road, Alabama, at the end of a dead-end road. We had lots of animals there, as our property backed up to my grandparents' hobby farm, so we had horses and cows and dogs and cats and rabbits and goats and pigs and geese. I remember talking to my parents at dinner one night about a calf I had seen earlier in the day. I had spent a good part of my afternoon chatting with the calf, who happily munched grass just on the other side of the barbed wire, which naturally meant we were now best friends and bonded for life. That night at the dinner table, I was suggesting names for the calf. I had settled on "Patsy" when my father interrupted me.

"We don't name the cows, son," he said, wiping his mouth on the worn cloth napkin.

"Why not?"

"Because we don't name the animals we are going to end up eating."

Dinner was, of course, hamburgers. Mine now hovered halfway to my mouth. I was old enough to know where our food came from, and I was totally fine eating animals. My grandmothers, who both loved to fish with me and my brothers, firmly believed that any fish big enough to have eyeballs was big enough to clean and eat. And when I shot my first dove off a power line with a single-shot .410, Dad helped me clean the bird and drop it straight into the fryer. But the realization that Patsy might better be named Patty had never dawned on me. I could eat a cow, but I could not eat Patsy. I started a mental inventory of every animal on the property. Which had names? Obviously, the dogs were safe. The black lab named Judge and the golden retriever named Soda were loved by our parents as fiercely as the children were. The goat was despised by my mother because every time we forgot to close the door, he would run inside and poop and then run back out. But he came to us with a name, so Fred the goat was probably safe. Our goose we called Guard Goose because it would chase strangers, honking and hissing so menacingly that even giant country boys would leap back into their pickups. "Was that a real enough name not to eat him?" I wondered. Regardless, I made a mental note to name all the animals tomorrow that I would rather not eat, and I finished my burger. It was my first real lesson on the power of naming.

The second lesson I got in naming came later, probably early high school, when my own name became an issue. Being the oldest son in my generation on my father's side of the family tree, I inherited the masculine family names in more detail than did my two younger brothers, my older girl cousins, and my younger male cousins. I not only got the traditional last name of my father's line, Butler, but I also got the middle name of Sim, which has been passed through male members of my father's family for generations. I have not always been thrilled about this name. For one thing, "Butler" was ripe for playground taunts. For years, I was Sim Butthole, Sim Butter, and Sim Butt. I don't remember being particularly upset by these nicknames, though, and eventually it was my middle name that became the real nuisance. Although many of my family members have "Sim" as their middle name, my parents decided to call me Sim instead of William, my first name, or some variation of that, like Will or Bill. My father, for instance, was Albert Sim Butler and went by Al. Likewise, his grandfather, Henry Sim, went by Henry.

As an adult, I like the name Sim, and I like going by it, even though it's my middle name. For one thing, it helps me quickly identify telemarketers, spammers, and other hucksters who make the mistake of addressing me as "William" on the phone. Moreover, the uniqueness of "Sim" always helped break the ice with someone new, with the "what an interesting name" and "where does your name come from" lines offering soft landing spots in those awkward moments of introduction.

But as a kid, uniqueness came with issues, the most obvious of which was an assumption by those older than myself that I had gotten my name wrong. Often, after I introduced myself, adults would think I had mispronounced my own name and would inquire, "Did you say 'Sam'?" No, sorry, adult, but I have learned my name and know how to say it. But at least you are asking. More often, adults would run with whatever name was closest to what they assumed I meant. Often called Jim, Tim, and Sims, I got into the habit of answering to anything that was close. This would bother me far more than "Sim Butt." Adults messing up my name felt like they were not trying, listening, or caring, and I then had to figure out how to interact with that person.

And if the middle and last names weren't enough trouble, my first name caused issues as well. Excited that I was the first male child on that side but worried that I may be the only one for that generation, my parents named me after both my grandfathers by making my first name "William," my mother's father's first name. This was not such a bad name until two years later, when my next brother arrived, and my parents reached into the great-grandfather name pot for his name. Now, with two sons, both the grandfathers and the great-grandfathers had title lineage embodied in our generation. Of course, when their third baby boy arrived five years later, my parents were out of ancestral names. As my mother tells it, "We were trying to have a girl." Instead of just picking a name they liked, they decided to name their last child after my maternal grandfather (again), so he became William Edward Waters Butler. A great name, no doubt, but my parents now had two boys named "William Something Butler." So even if we wanted to, neither of us could go by our first name. While it only really became a problem when we had to show our identifications at the airport or both had an open tab at a bar, we gave our parents a lot of crap for a lack of creativity. Even still, I think my brothers and I like our names, mostly for whom they remind us of.

Names carry weight because they are a near-constant reminder of not only who you are but also from whom you follow. Here in the Deep South, we ask strangers, "Who are your people?" When you live in a small town, you assume that you have a connection with strangers, which sometimes means you treat them better. If I live in the country and I call a plumber, this person might be my only plumber option, and I probably know his momma, so I better be kind or I'm going to hear about it from my momma. When my friends around the country ask me what I like about the South, this is my first thought. I get how we can be good to one another here, how we have to be. You don't get angry and honk at the tractor barely doing five miles an hour. The farmer's name is Paul; he grew up with everyone you are named after, and he will get out of your way as soon as he can. Living in small, rural spaces provides me with a sense of community and the comfort that comes with it, which we Southerners often project into our bigger cities as well, with varying results.

I remember how differently this concept affected me personally when I was a teenager. When I started to drive and would get out and about on my own, people would recognize my name and ask if I was related to my grandfather. His name was Maxwell Sim Butler, and he went by Mac Sim. Every few years, his name would be on posters all over Montgomery County when he ran for reelection for sheriff. His thirty-six-year term in office, from 1955 to 1991, is the second-longest streak in the state. I was eleven years old when he left office, so most of the memories I have of him are grandfatherly, like picking plums off his trees and scooping handfuls of pecans off the ground in his yard, which he'd crack for me. But I also remember him as Sheriff Butler, complete with a chocolate

Stetson cowboy hat, as he finished out his law enforcement career in the 1980s and early 1990s. I do not have memories of the rest of his career, the parts that were crucial to most everyone else. He died with those and left me to do research.

While he was sheriff, and I was a kid, I loved being around him. As his first grandson, who shared his name, I was his shadow whenever I could be. I often ended up at his office in the jail across from the courthouse. With a ten-year-old in tow, those were obviously pretty quiet days for my grandfather. We did not pull anyone over, transport any prisoners, or do anything official. He was on the clock, wearing his dark-brown uniform, including the star-shaped badge with the state of Alabama in the middle, but if I was there, he did not wear his pistol. In fact, the first time I saw him in uniform with a gun was in an old picture in the paper, first published decades before, during the Civil Rights Movement.

There are always parts of your family that you know about long before you know enough to put it all together. Children see their parents be ugly to each other for years and are still surprised when the marriage officially dissolves. Being with my grandfather as sheriff, having him give me a tour of the jail, even closing me in a cell and pretending to leave me there, or even being at his home with him, where he taught me to saddle a horse, gave me the thousands of close-up details without the distance needed to see the whole picture.

As an adult, I'm still working to reconcile what I know of him with what he did in a time before I knew him. I do this partially because he was my grandfather, and I love him deeply. Maybe I do it because law enforcement and race continue to be mired in cycles of violence and fear. Mostly, I think about my grandfather because I have his name and the weight it comes with.

At fifteen, I was getting my learner's permit at the local state troopers' office. There was an older Black woman behind the counter, and when I told her my name for my permit, she stopped and gave me a hard look. Not mean, but penetrative. "Are you kin to Sheriff Mac Sim Butler?" she asked, holding my eyes.

"Yes, ma'am, he's my grandfather."

She held my gaze over half-moon glasses for a long beat, in one of those "tell me what you did before I have to find it out" looks.

That's how I knew this was serious. People often knew my grandfather and were happy to tell me how they knew him or why they wanted to know him. They would smile and be warm. I knew what to do with folks like that. But she was measuring me against what she knew of him. That was new for me, and profoundly unsettling.

"He is a good man," she finally said, while still holding my gaze.

"Yes, ma'am," I said again, and we went back to business.

I got my permit and left with one of my parents, and nothing was totally amiss, but in a palpable way I was back on the farm. I knew how the burger was made, but I had named the calf already. My grandfather was sheriff of Montgomery County, Alabama, during the Civil Rights Movement, and he would always stop and tie my shoe when a lace was loose. He was a white man of significant power during a time when the heroes were not the men with badges. In this case, I had no idea how the woman behind the counter knew my grandfather. She did not tell me, and I did not ask. But it was clear she had lived alongside him in some way that would be private to her. I would not know what her experience was exactly, but I would be a reflection of it. Whatever my grandfather did or didn't do was a direct reflection on me. I felt that, and the link I would always have with him, because of my name.

I'm not totally sure how the rest of the world learns about the Civil Rights Movement in the United States, but in Alabama in the 1990s, as a young white man with plenty of everything, civil rights education consisted of two important themes: (1) segregation was wrong, the violence to sustain it was abhorrent, and it took place in our backyard; and (2) we fixed it, it's over, and we wish people would quit bringing it up. This was particularly convenient for young white children like me. First, we got to admit that that shit was not cool. We were allowed to find the level of disgust, horror, and self-reflection we were comfortable with, call it empathy, and then turn around and say, "We aren't like that anymore." We could then replace any thought of culpability for modern inequities with the misguided belief that a few bad apples abused their power long ago.

Having my grandfather's name changed that calculous for me. I could not disassociate from the Civil Rights Movement because a man at the center of that fight around justice, race, and power not only looks like me but shares my name.

I did my research. In the beginning, I used the internet to research my grandfather's past like a teenager using pornography to figure out how sex works. There was a potential for shame, but crouching over a dimly lit laptop in secret felt private and shielded me from most of the fear of those feelings. I looked only long enough to know what I was looking at, and then I moved on, claiming satisfaction. It's only in hindsight that we understand that such fictions mask deeper truths.

From first glance, the broad picture of the struggle was one that did not really include my grandfather. I took comfort in that lack of inclusion. I told myself a simple story: He must not have been a terrible sheriff. History asks us to remember the names of the villains. People know the names of other law enforcement leaders in Alabama at that time, like the Birmingham commissioner of public safety, Eugene "Bull" Connor, who set dogs and firehoses on peaceful protestors. They've heard about Sheriff Jim Clark in Selma, whose deputies attacked Reverend John Lewis and other marchers on the Edmund Pettus Bridge on the day later dubbed "Bloody Sunday." People know about the state troopers and FBI agents who aided and abetted white supremacists in bombing churches, homes, and buses. The heroes, like Rosa Parks and the Reverend Dr. Martin Luther King Jr., are more well known, and rightfully so. A little knowledge can often be mistaken for understanding, so while I knew my grandfather was not a Bull Connor, I originally accepted his lack of villainy as good enough. I spared myself some potential shame and guilt when convenient and consequently set myself up for the mistakes that followed from a lack of understanding. But that lack of understanding came into sharp focus as my family grew.

I felt so strongly that my grandfather the sheriff be remembered that I named my firstborn child after him: Mac Sim Butler. "Mac," meaning "son of" Sim, was a play on words, a play on history making, and our first inside joke, I had hoped. We kept it a secret from the family until the birth, and the explanation of it was part of the first conversation I had with my child there in the hospital nursery. It was celebrated within our family, and it was a mistake.

I wish I could claim that I had no way of knowing any better, but that's not true at all. I was absolutely prepared to get this lesson on naming right. In a college literature class at the University of Alabama, I breezed through lessons on how naming characters shapes the narrative, how it's the most powerful tool an author has to bend a character toward (or away) from an audience. In graduate school, I read how philosophers like Michel Foucault considered naming a tool of hegemony and power and a way of wielding control over public perception through labels that restrict and regulate those who are saddled with the denotations and connotations of those names. As a budding academic, I could make complicated arguments about the impact and influence that particular names—of people, places, events, and concepts—have on cultures and politics. I have done some self-reflection, both the coordinated, thoughtful, and productive kind and the less helpful, navel-gazing type, to try to understand how the forces I bear in these spaces, like my whiteness, my gender, and my privilege, complicate my own power to name and to critique the naming of others. And while I can talk that talk and walk that walk in my professional life, I have a tendency to shut off that side of my brain in my personal life. So the next lesson in the power of naming never took into account these academic overtones. Consequently, and appropriately, my first mistake as a parent was the first decision I got to make as a parent.

How bad a mistake I made is up for interpretation, and I'll let you be the judge of it, because the relationship between someone and what they are called is a contested space. It's often the first interaction we have with someone, and, like the handshake, it depends on coordination and cooperation. I tell you my name and I expect you to use it. If you don't, we have a problem. My wife watches this exchange play itself out every time I go in to a doctor's office. They call me back with "Mr. Butler?," which, in most cases, makes sense. But I have an educational degree that means, formally, it should be "Dr. Butler." But insisting on being called Dr. Butler with a PhD in a room full of medical doctors doesn't fit the context. So I always answer the call for "Mr. Butler?" with "Call me 'Sim.'" That's a compromise I can work with.

If they don't call me Sim? Well, I get grumpy. I rant on the way home. And I make a mental note to put that person into the "Sim Butt" category. Luckily for me, that's the extent of it. It may be disrespectful, but it's never dangerous for me. And so I assumed that no danger existed for anyone. But for folks who change their names to reflect who they are, authentically, on the inside, there are real perils when introductions are contested. When a transgender person says "Call me by my name," danger lies just below the surface. A refusal to do so means a public outing, and the chance of spontaneous violence drastically increases. A study published in the *American Journal of Public Health* in March 2021 confirms that transgender folks face drastically elevated levels of assault, murder, and harassment. This violence can hinge on the simple discovery that someone is trans. Imagine if every introduction carried the gravity of potential violence. All because a parent guesses wrong during the naming.

I named my first child after my grandfather, and I'm afraid it might get her killed someday. My child, after six years of going by Mac, of sporting short hair and a shorter temper, of stuttering attempts at self-expression and violent expressions of self-harm, of dress-up, always dress-up, of mermaids and princesses in peril, my child could not contain herself any longer. A month before her seventh birthday, she told us, voice shaking, that she was "a girl in her heart, a girl in her mind, even though she had a boy body." She didn't yet know the word *transgender*. She didn't know that she would later change her name, transition socially, or seek medical care for gender dysphoria, and in doing so would leave behind a frustrated and fearful little boy for a vibrant, joyful little girl. For the next seven years, we watched this child blossom into someone special.

Then, at thirteen years old, she, like her great-grandfather for whom she was originally named, was thrust into a fight for justice in Alabama. Starting in 2022, our home state began passing a slew of laws limiting the rights of transgender children, like my daughter. She can no longer play sports, use the appropriate bathroom, or receive the medical care she needs to treat her gender dysphoria. I used to gently tease her when she was little for saying "When I grow up, I'm going to be a mommy" instead of a daddy, another mistake on my part. To pay for that mistake, the law that makes us all felons—my wife, myself, and my child's wonderful doctors—for following the best medical practices for transgender children went into effect on Mother's Day of 2022.

See what I did there? I started talking about what I did wrong as a parent but almost immediately jumped into the injustices done to me and my family years later. Self-reflection sucks. It's very hard for me to do it truthfully without remembering what I did and continue to do wrong. The problem I've made for myself has very little to do with the actual names that link my family like any other family. The problem is about authority. The story of my daughter needs to be told, particularly right now in this country. And yet, the assumption that I should have the authority to tell the stories, to name the characters and describe their positions in the struggle for justice in Alabama, could do much to illustrate the way that history making shapes the modern-day culture and politics of a place. I have to rectify my spot, my position, my perspective, and my story within the confines of which stories are mine and which are not.

Like, when it became apparent that my daughter needed a new name, she picked Marina. Objectively, it's a beautiful name, and considering her childhood obsession with mermaids, I should have seen it coming. But in our family, a marina is where you park a boat. So a negotiation broke out. "How about *this*?" I'd say, or "Your grandmother was named *this*," I'd suggest. And the whole time, I'm thinking, "This is why we don't let children name themselves!" Because children's motivations, their reasoning, and their tastes are not ours. And yet, here I was reverting back to Sim Buttface. The nickname was not for me, but for my classmates, which is why one can never nickname themself. Attempting to name my daughter again was an attempt to reassert my authority to name.

I could not name my child again, as I did not know her well enough to get it right the first time. So I had to let go and let her tell me what she needed to be called to feel like herself, regardless of whether it fit into our family tree or aligned with my expectations of what a name should be. And she has a beautiful name. What it is and how she came to it is her story. Someday, I hope she tells it.

I wish I could end this story there. Not only would I save myself the embarrassment of having to admit all the other mistakes I've made parenting a trans kid, but I could relish the pleasure of patiently watching my daughter grow, mature, and flourish. Parents want to raise their children to someday face down dragons. But for my family, the dragons have come early. When Alabama banned gender-affirming health care in 2022, it forced my family to choose between advocating for ourselves, our home, and the health of my daughter or getting the hell out. Alabama was home. We built careers, communities, and our family within the culture. I firmly believed that being in Alabama was good for my kids and good for the people who got to know my kids. But the days of picking and choosing our battles, of being private but not secretive about our family's gender makeup, suddenly ended. Advocacy is inherently public. As we talked to lawyers about suing the state to block the law from going into effect, it became clear that we might not have been able to shield our daughter, then thirteen, from the lawsuit. She would have to be on the amicus brief. She might have even have to testify. The dragon was at the doorstep, but was she ready to fight it herself?

Left without that answer, as any parent would, I looked for ways to advocate for her. Talking the people we knew through the problems with the laws was easy. Most people were curious and supportive. Once, asking a close relative for advice on how to legally challenge the law that aimed to ban gender-affirming health care for youth, he pressed on the particulars. Even as he worked through the specifics of law, he reflected, "I read that this law is to prevent unnecessary genital surgeries on kids."

"The surgeries mentioned in the law don't exist, at least not in Alabama," I countered. "But in reasoning that they could exist as a part of extreme care for a transgender child and should therefore be banned, the law removes all access to reasonable affirming care, even types that are totally reversible, noninvasive, and explicitly categorized as best practice according to leading medical authorities." We all came from a hunting family, so I tried an analogy. "Hell, that's like outlawing hunting animals with horns to save the unicorns!"

I've had similar conversations with loving family members, close friends, acquaintances, and even strangers over the years. I've found that the logical arguments and reasoning against transphobic laws are plentiful but unrelatable. Telling our family's story, I hope, bridges that gap for those who have not interacted or will not interact with transgender, gender-diverse, or nonbinary people. If you know my daughter, you probably already know what these laws do to me and my family. But for everyone else, for everyone on the fringe of this issue, or beginning down a similar path, I have made the choice to tell our story.

From there, a new question emerges. If telling our story is a form of advocacy, what do I call my daughter, the subject of this narrative? Names are power, after all, but whose? How do I leave her the space to define herself, while simultaneously advocating for her?

And here comes the first major dilemma for me as I write this story. I have to name my child again, and every option I have is fraught with peril. Here are my choices: (1) I can use only "my daughter" and her pronouns, (2) I can use her old name, (3) I can use a pseudonym, or (4) I can use her new name. All of these choices have positives and negatives. Believe me, I've cycled through them through the years. But let's put your parenting chops to the test and see what you think of my options.

Choice number one works in bursts. It's great for signaling the gender transition for people who might have known my daughter before her transition. But it's tricky because I have two daughters, so there can also be confusion as to which I mean. On top of that, pronouns and genealogical labels are boring and flat. They evade the issue at hand, which is naming, and ignore the purpose of this book. I need you to know my daughter. When I tell you the story about her creatively refusing to play soccer or sneaking out at night to sled, I want you to be able to picture her. For that, you need a name. Names make us familiar. Without one, she's a nonentity, a statistic, a mystery. So option one is out.

Option two: I can use her old name. It's the name we originally printed on her birth certificate, I've acknowledged it previously as an important family name, and it's a name she answered to for six and a half years. While it doesn't feel right at all to use her old name for her now, many of the stories I'm planning on telling about her are from when she didn't go by that name. How will that work in the storytelling? Is it as authentic to what happened as the audience needs it to be? Sure, the old name represents, for her, six and a half years of turmoil and misunderstanding and a desperate fight to express herself. But aren't those necessary ingredients in her story?

The easy answer here is that one should never use the old name, a practice dubbed *deadnaming*. The academic writer and debater in me pushes back. Deadnaming specifically means using the old, retired name of a transperson against their wishes in the present. It is a huge act of disrespect and a deplorable tactic. That's not what would be happening here. Recalling a history when things were different is no form of disrespect, I could argue, but an acknowledgment of the brave steps toward actualization and fulfillment.

The argument I can't get around is that using her old name would feel like deadnaming, even for me. Long before my daughter came out, I was working with a graduate student and community activist, Tiffany, and we were collaborating on some research around recent public narratives on coming out as trans. Chaz Bono had just finished competing on *Dancing with the Stars*, and, as the first out transgender contestant, his journey was heavily chronicled. But while this meeting was set to discuss research, Tiffany was not interested in discussing new projects. After some gentle prodding, we got to the why: She was grieving the loss of another transgender person in Birmingham who had recently been murdered.

"To make matters worse, I heard about it on the news," she said, and she went stiff.

"I'm so sorry," I said, assuming that learning an acquaintance had died through the news signaled a lack of communication with others, like family or friends, which is what had caused Tiffany to go rigid. But there was more to it.

"I worked in a newsroom for years. Do you know, when a transgender person is murdered, and reporters call the police to get the story, the police only release the deadname." This was the first I had heard the term. She continued, but her hands were gripping the café table as if she might flip it. "They can't even use the person's real name when they are standing over the body. They might as well whip out their pricks and piss on her."

My mind raced. Why would they use the old name? Is it a legal issue? Are they bound to go by names on legal forms? What are the cultural impacts of this? Wouldn't this hamper the ability to monitor and track targeted crimes against transgender community members, like hate crimes or serial killers, or even accurately tally the homicides committed against trans folks? But Tiffany pulled me back.

"When you are trans, you come into this life, and no one knows who you are. You have to tell them, 'No, call me by my name.' And then, when you die, you can't tell them that anymore, and they go back to calling you by your deadname again. Like you never lived at all."

Door number three: I could use a pseudonym. Appealingly, it aims to keep her identity secret. As a parent, I am desperate to keep her safe, and we have lived in places and times where I am constantly afraid of who will find her and punish her for being herself. I stand outside the bathroom at supermarkets, waiting for her to finish going potty and pumping myself up for a physical altercation if someone pulls her out by her ear. Bathrooms are terribly dangerous places for trans folks of all ages.

Another positive of the pseudonym, I pick the name to call her for this manuscript. Like a fiction writer, I could shape her character with the power of naming. What would be the most adorable, likeable, or, perhaps as important, forgivable name I could conjure? What name would be universal enough that she would feel familiar without making her feel made up? I could choose a moniker that serves the narrative. But would it be serving her? Sure, I can claim to do it for her own good, and it might benefit the story, but only if I can tell it better than she already has. Which I can't. Nor do I need to. This story does not need to be better than it is. It simply needs to be told.

That leaves me with option four, to use her name. This would be the one she picked for herself, that I got no say in, and that would identify her to both family and strangers. Using her name would give you the fullest picture of her. But there is massive risk with this choice. We live in a world and culture where bullying happens in person and digitally from around the globe. It's an environment where the reaction of many is to lash out to cause physical or emotional harm to those they simply disagree with, using doxing and swatting as tools of degradation, humiliation, and violence. And being against the rights of transgender people has become a political marker in this country as well. In 2022, the American Civil Liberties Union counted 469 anti-LGBTQ+ bills introduced in state legislatures. These bills are mostly introduced as a line in the sand in the conservative culture war, drumming up the base by targeting the already stigmatized. Would you make your child a target in such conditions?

I would expose her to people who want to do evil to her as well as outing her to everyone else too. College admissions personnel, high school classmates, postal service workers, and our next-door neighbor. Everyone who reads this book and comes across her in a situation in which she has to introduce herself would know that she is transgender. She could no longer pick and choose who knows and who doesn't know something that is immensely private. Once I use her name here, I rob her of that power. I wonder, when she goes in for her driver's license and gets that knowing look from the lady in the half-moon glasses, will she want that power back? Once she's out, she can't reclaim that anonymity. Publishing her name means she can no longer be stealthy, and I know that stealth functions not only as a privacy screen that can be comforting but also as an often-necessary camouflage for transgender folks. The last thing I want to do is reduce my daughter's safety measures, to remove her protections. That means that this choice is out too.

For those of you keeping score at home, all of my options are losers. But if you've been paying attention, you knew before I began that I was asking the wrong question. They are all bad choices for me, but that's because I assumed I was the one who got to choose in the first place. I learned that lesson the first time I screwed it up. So I asked her. I laid out all the options, and I walked her through the negatives and the positives. And she asked that I call her by her name.

"You want me to use your name?" We were walking by the river while we talked about it. These walks are common practice. We hike or walk along the river while her sister is at climbing team practice. Most times we take turns talking in these walks. When it's her turn, she tells me stories, long rambling odysseys with made-up characters and their superpowered adventures. Every day for as long as I can remember, she finds time to make up epic stories involving science fiction or fantasy characters, often playing in those worlds either by herself or with friends. When it's my turn to talk, I ask her complex questions. She loves a riddle. Simple riddles are my favorite, like "I am something, but I am nothing. Put me in a bucket and I'll make it lighter." But she prefers complicated riddles, with a handful of clues to decipher and some sort of story, like the one where a father and son have a car accident, the father dies on the way to hospital, and the doctor says, "I can't operate on this child, he's my son!" If I don't have a riddle, I pose brainteasers or vexing questions. Every now and then, I ask her something serious, like this time. I told her about my choices, and she thought about it but answered swiftly.

"Use my real name."

"Are you sure?" She had spoken with finality, but I was hoping she would change her mind. This was not the first or the last time that particular hope would fail me.

"Yes," she said. I could tell she was already losing patience with me because she had picked up a stick and begun to use it like a magic wand. She pointed it at me. "If you are writing about me, you should use my name."

One of the hardest things to do as a parent, I have learned, is to treat your child with dignity and respect while they are clearly trying to cast a spell on you. "If I use your name, everyone who reads this will know that you are transgender. Your name tells them that."

"If you don't use my name, then will people know me?" she asked over her shoulder, because she had scurried toward a bigger knotty branch up ahead and just off the path that would make an excellent staff.

I started to answer, but she was far enough away that I would have had to shout. Instead, I pondered her question. I'm not sure exactly what she meant when she asked it, but the answer seems clear enough. People will not know her unless I use her name.

And then she was back, holding the stick to me because she likes the twig-sized branches snapped off, and she prefers I do it. "And what will people call me if you don't use my name?" she asked.

There is the heart of it. As much as I ache to protect her, I have to understand that the first and most important way to do that is by supporting her. She picked her name because she feels it represents her. Omitting her name means that anyone can then decide what to call her. Even subconsciously, without a name or even with a pseudonym, a reader may fill in the gap with a name of their own choosing to better understand the story. I would substitute her power to choose what she is called for the marginal protection of partial anonymity.

Life with a transgender child centers on how best to support and protect the child, just like parenting a cisgender one, but the choices I've made over the years have always been diluted by fear. Few of the choices have been easy or straightforward. Many come with risks and advocacy necessitates exposure. This book chronicles my having to learn these lessons again and again. Luckily for me, my daughter is a patient teacher.

When I first began writing this book, I was prepared to honor her wishes, but in that small window of time, from writing to publication, the world has gotten a lot scarier for the tiny population of transgender folks in America. Over almost a decade, our family's journey has ballooned from being solely about our private lives into being part of a community whose rights to health care, education, and government recognition are increasingly under threat, becoming arguments heard in front of the U.S. Supreme Court. This has led not only to new legal challenges, but also social ones. People have been emboldened to follow their leaders, entrenching dangerous stereotypes and justifying violence against an already vulnerable population. So here I am, choosing to use a pseudonym for my daughter in this story of her life, hoping it helps keep her alive. Someday, maybe I'll get this naming thing right, but, for now, like any parent would, I do only what I think is best for her. Let me introduce you to my daughter. Please call her Kate.

2

Memorabilia

When people learn that my daughter Kate is trans and has been out as trans since before she turned seven years old, they want to know how she told us. Over the years, I've found that this is a pretty safe starting point for most people for two reasons. First, coming out is a known phenomenon within and beyond the LGBTQ+ community and typically involves unique and powerful moments of vulnerability, acceptance, or rejection that help noncommunity members relate to the struggles queer people face. Even when straight, cisgender folks don't have to come out as straight, there are parts of that type of struggle that resonate. For one thing, the thought that family members would reject each other based on who and how they love is terrifying. For another, having to talk personally about sex, sexuality, and sexual desires, thanks to its taboo-ness, is not easy for even the straightest of straight people. But add in a touch of cultural norm busting, and that conversation becomes a minefield of snap moral judgments, knee-jerk stigmatization, and disgust-fueled avoidance. But I think that people who want to be supportive but have never had to come out are also working through their own hang-ups around getting it on and are learning how not to react. Sex, and feeling good and safe and loved during sex, are highly personal things. So hearing about someone who wants to do it differently from the way you want to do it can come with that first thought of "I don't want that," which is natural and fine, but it's not terribly supportive, loving, or attentive. And it can, if not reasoned through, be faulty evidence used to reject the other person. This would be the same if straight people were a little more open and honest about how they do sex, since there is plenty of shaming for practically every form of intercourse that doesn't involve the most puritanical of methods and relationships. But we don't make swingers publicly confess the way we do queer people.

As a parent, I'm working through possible analogies to help people along. While most people have sex and like sex and can therefore find a reference point for the concept of loving whom you love, coming out as transgender has a much less obvious connection point for me to reference. This is the second reason that Kate's coming-out story functions as an important introduction to our family. For Kate, coming out involved a self-expression of identity detached from sexuality. Whereas a gay man bucks cultural norms about what love and sex should look like, a trans person's coming out can involve breaking conceptions of how a body's anatomy works to define who we are. As a cisgender person, I can confidently say that most of us are very comfortable in the idea that our physical bodies are both an expression and a representation of who we feel we are. In the plainest of terms, cisgender people who have a penis identify as a male, man, or boy, and cisgender people with a vagina identify as female, woman, or girl. This penis = boy and vagina = girl binary is comfortable in its ease and widespread acceptance. It's the first reference point, confirmed at birth, proclaimed exuberantly by a doctor, and stamped on government documents not long after. And since most of us feel good about that anatomy-to-identity linkage, since it affirms how many of us feel, this argument has become a cultural truth. Coming out as transgender challenges this norm the same way coming out as lesbian challenges norms around sex. We all have feelings around sex we can use to connect across the spectrum of sexuality. But transgender folks lack a reference point for cisgender folks. This is why people ask me about Kate's coming out. Most people are looking for that connection point. With those two pieces in mind, I have a particular story I tell. It goes like this:

> Kate came out to us on a hot and hazy afternoon in July in the living room of our house on the Cahaba River in Birmingham. That summer, we had a daily babysitter, Jasmine, who would come over to watch the kids or take them on an adventure while Rachel was at her physical therapy clinic and I worked from home. Jasmine was our kids' favorite babysitter because she was kind and patient and played with them, but also because she would occasionally break the no-electronics rule and let them watch *Teen Beach*. But one day, as we were saying goodbye for the evening, Jasmine announced, "I think someone has something to tell you . . ."

Before I go any further, I think it's important to know that the story I tell is as true as I can stand it to be. By that, I mean it's exactly how I remember it happening, not necessarily how it actually happened. That's by accident and the result of an imperfect memory. In addition, in the practiced version of the story, I'm leaving out important context. This is on purpose. One benefit is that it fits the cultural expectations of a coming-out story. What most people expect is a singular moment of confession. For years, I had this same misconception, so I know how to tell the story that way. I have it practiced, and it meets expectations, so for short interactions it works well.

The second reason is more selfish. Coming out, I have learned, is not a one-time event. It is like a group of people in the know. It starts with the individual and self-recognition and then grows, more fragile than glass, to include those closest and most likely to be supportive. But in telling our story cat's-out-of-the-bag style, I'm showing you a tree in great detail to distract you from the forest, because the forest is a scary place for me. To belabor the metaphor, the forest has monsters hiding in the dark, and they may be real, or they may be imagined. But even imagined monsters are real enough to scare you sometimes. My monsters formed from my fear of how to handle Kate's coming out. This fear came in two flavors. First, there is the fear that I was doing something wrong. I'll give you an example. We have a pair of wooden picture frames in our bedroom at the lake cabin. Both originally held pictures of our children at the lake. The one with a picture still in it shows my youngest daughter, Evelyn, about age four, looking up at the camera, wearing a bathing suit and my giant straw lake hat tilted back on her head. The sun off the water makes the lopsided bill look like a halo, which matches the wry smile on her face. It's a near-perfect picture, capturing the unprepped and delicate cuteness that shows when the unbridled joy of a particular stage of life stops for a moment to relish the comfort of being happy. I love that picture. It brings me about as much joy as the empty frame brings me shame. The other wooden frame used to hold a picture of Kate before she came out. In it, she has wrangled around seventeen pool noodles into a single flotation device and balances precariously on all of them. She is age six, on her belly, with her blond hair roguishly swept across her forehead as her head is tilted back toward the camera. You can tell as much by the look on her face as by anything else that the pile of foam noodles will not hold together for long, despite her outstretched and swaying arms and legs. It, too, was a take-the-picture-quickly-before-the-moment-is-gone type of photo. Two photos beside each other, each perfect moments in our children's lives. Evelyn's picture is still in the frame, but Kate's picture only lasted a couple of months because it was later that summer of that year that Kate came out to us as trans. One of the first things I did after she came out was purge the pictures of her as a boy.

Taking pictures out of frames is definitely not standard operating procedure, and it's probably not the healthy way to work through your child's gender journey. It was a lizard brain, knee-jerk reaction, an attempt to fix a problem that didn't actually exist. In my thinking, if you can call it that, I wanted to rid Kate of any reminder of a time before she had the words to express who she was on the inside and was mistaken as someone else. It turns out, I invented this problem to deal with the real one: Kate did a lot of her own coming out, but she was expecting us to do some of it along with her, maybe even for her. Old, precious pictures of her around the house forced me to have that conversation with every curious visitor, and it took me a while to live into that role. At six years old, my kid was searching for the words to explain what she felt. But every light bulb that came on for her on that journey was a flashbulb, brilliant and illuminating and sudden. She wanted more because the more she learned, the better she felt. But we had to be her interpreters, not for what she was experiencing or trying to express but to the rest of the world. Yet, we had no personal experience, no reference point for what she was experiencing, along with a fear that it would continue or reverse suddenly, and either way we would screw it up. It felt like hitting a moving target with a flying squirrel from a slingshot while blindfolded and drunkenly singing karaoke.

To make matters worse, I absurdly assumed I understood what coming out meant for a queer person. Give a person a fish, and they'll call themselves a Bassmaster. I am straight, but I had studied communication and queerness, published academic papers about media narratives centered on coming out in various public ways and forms, and felt that my academic understanding of this phenomenon prepared me for the day when one of my own children might come out to me. It didn't. I was not ready and had no understanding that buffered me from my lack of lived experience coupled with layers of white male arrogance. In fact, people would

Memorabilia

often hear about Kate's identity and say things like "Oh, she's so lucky to have you as a father," and nothing made me feel like more of a fraud: I was ill-prepared but confident, a terrible combination.

Worst still, I felt like my fraudulence had real consequences. My bones were telling me that not understanding something I was supposed to understand meant danger. Have you ever walked up on an apex predator in the wild, like a grizzly bear? I stumbled across the biggest alligator I'd ever seen while hunting turkeys in a swamp. That damn dinosaur was twelve feet long and had massive white jowls that made it look like he was resting his head on a pillow. Like a fool, I pulled out my phone to take a picture, and he slid into the water and cut the distance between us to fifteen feet before I could cuss properly. You meet up with an animal that can eat you in the wild, and you suddenly realize you are dangerously out of your element. As Kate came out, there I was, again feeling that same sense of dumbfounding helplessness. I still feel that way sometimes. As I write this chapter, I struggle with how to talk about Kate before she was Kate. The historically accurate story notes that Kate legally changed her name, but how do I tell the story of Kate before Kate? Before she identified as a "she," she answered to "he." Does it complicate the story? You bet your ass it does. But, more importantly, it highlights my discomfort with my role in her coming out as transgender.

"I think someone has something to tell you" typically meant trouble in our house. My wife and I both assumed something was broken beyond repair, the dog's hair had been cut, or the garden hose had been brought into the house again. Our oldest had a knack for destruction, not in a malicious way, but by playing too hard. When we were moving in, for example, her excitement over the new home had her racing from room to room until she leapt up on the kitchen table and swung on the chandelier. She got one good lift and swing, and as she descended again, the momentum pulled the light fixture free, dropping her butt-first back onto the table. By the time we heard the crash and entered the room, she was trying to simultaneously unravel herself from the debris and stop grinning. So when the babysitter announces "It's confession time!," we are doing a quick inventory of fragile items in the home. But this time, the look on my child's face was not one of mischief or remorse. I saw resolve.

When our kid came out, we had emotional steps we had to work through. I don't know for sure, but I'm willing to bet this is true for everyone who has a child come out as queer. What those steps are, and how they feel to work through, can be as varied as the experiences and makeups of each family. Working through these personal steps sets the pace for the practical steps because the first person your child is trying to convince to accept them is you. That doesn't mean you are the first person to know; they might tell another confidant first. But you are probably the first person they tell whose acceptance is paramount to them. But here's the thing: They can't actually convince you to accept them. At least, they can't do it by themselves. I've taught persuasion for over a decade, and I firmly believe that persuasion is a collaborative endeavor, meaning no one can do it to someone else without their participation in the process. Any child attempting to come out, attempting to persuade a parent that they made incorrect assumptions about their child, needs a compassionate and willing listener. Especially when it's a child doing the convincing, it's so easy to dismiss their story as beyond their understanding. In the beginning, I believed my process of understanding to be logical, analytical, and rational. I would listen to new information but put together the evidence myself in order to draw a conclusion, especially when that conclusion differed from my original one. When Kate first came out to me, I told myself that the age of my child made them an unreliable narrator, even of their own story, and that I would need to investigate this coming out as a process to accept it. It took me a while to understand that this stage of coming out is really about coming *in*. I was invited into confidence, and it was my job to accept, not scrutinize, that invitation.

Of course, I had to learn this lesson the hard way. One time I told our go-to coming-out story while sitting on a panel at a small rural liberal arts college in a town hall on transgender and gender-diverse issues. Everyone else on the panel was an expert, either through vocation or lived experience, had worked for decades as advocates for the LGBTQ+ community in the region, so when we got to the Q and A portion at the end, I was surprised when a set of questions were directed to me. A student with purple hair raised their hand and asked, "How do you get your parents to understand like you seem to?" I had no idea how to answer. Immediately, I felt like my fraudulence was exposed. If I truly supported, accepted, and affirmed my trans kid, I should be able to tell others how to do the same. My despair must have been plain on my face, because the student rephrased and asked again, "I mean, how do I get my parents to accept me?" They were on the verge of tears now. All I wanted to do in that moment was to dispense wisdom, to say something both comforting and prophetic, and I had nothing. I was not comfortable about how I felt about my child's trans journey, or maybe I wasn't totally confident about how I was handling it, so how could I possibly outline how to make another adult feel comfortable? I did say something about how parents develop expectations for how their kids' lives will turn out and how we become fearful when we think our kids will have a tough path, but even as I said the words, I knew I was missing the mark. Deep down, even as I practiced affirmation, I harbored the feelings that drive some parents to reject their LGBTQ+ kids.

My doubts, which I was masking with my analytical process, exposed a much more emotional response I was not yet willing to address. I actively grieved the aspects of my child's future life that she would not have because of being transgender. I felt shame for that grief. I still have anger and frustration when I encounter misunderstandings, uninvited advice, or uninformed opinions about raising a trans kid. So like any well-meaning and terrified parent, I set out to convince myself, because I refused to let my child do it for me.

We started with therapists, both one for my wife Rachel and myself and one for Kate. Our therapist was gentle and was set to let us eventually figure things out on our own. Kate's was less so. She was a play therapist, and we quietly hoped Kate would play with her Legos and pet her dog and forget about the whole thing. The opposite happened. With the right questions and a safe space, Kate articulated clearly her gender dysphoria and had an adult advocate with the credentials to move things in the proper direction and at the proper speed. After a few sessions, Kate had broached the subject of changing her name from the one we had originally picked to Kate. The therapist pulled me aside at the end of the session to show me a picture Kate had drawn. A lovely scene in crayon, and at the top, the name "Kate" was clearly written by my child. By now, you know about my hang-ups with names, but at the time, I didn't. "What do you think this means?" I asked. Thank God child therapists are patient souls.

"Well," she said, "it means that your child wants to be called 'Kate.'"

"Okay, but do you think they understand the ramification of a decision like that?" I asked, because I thought I understood better, at the time. "Children at this age can't comprehend the real-world and long-term consequences of something like this, right?"

"Whether she understands the future or not is irrelevant. She is offering a glimpse into how she sees herself right now. Don't look past that."

And that's exactly what I was doing. I was looking past the moment into the future, actively grieving the life my child was not going to have. None of the gendered rites of passage I had pictured, like wearing a tux to prom, were going to happen the way I had thought they would. My little boy was not going to grow up to be a man, and I felt unmoored from life. Even before I was faced with a child with gender dysphoria, I felt unprepared as a parent, like I hardly knew how to teach a young human how to take even the easiest life path possible. And the alternative was terrifying. I had no idea what the future held, but I knew it would involve stigmatization, fear, and disgust from total strangers and, perhaps, even loved ones. But my child moved me along. "She is offering a glimpse into how she sees herself," the therapist's words, resonated. "Don't look past that." Was I doing the best thing for my child here, in the present? Was I going to be loving and supportive as we continued to figure this out together? Yes, I could do that, and it was the foundation I needed to move forward. I was never able to predict the future, even when I thought my kid would grow up to be a man, so while the future scared me more now, I did not need to know the future to proceed into it. Luckily for us all, Kate did not wait for me to get over that fear before leading us from the foundation of the present into the future.

"Go ahead," Jasmine coaxed. "Tell them what you told me at lunch." She was on one couch, and we were on the other. My beautiful little boy made eye contact with me and said, "I am a girl in my heart."

You may be the first person your child comes out to, but once you've come to grips with your new understanding of your child, your work is hardly over, because you now have an important role in how that circle of support expands. The center of that circle is the person who is coming out, and just beyond them is you, and then their immediate family, biological as well as chosen. The ironic part, of course, is that you've done this part before. What used to be a private moment at a sonogram appointment and among family and friends our culture has monetized into social media performances. Gender revealing has become ritualized in such a way that people can feel pressured, encouraged, and normal in constructing extravagant celebrations involving everything from clandestine baked goods to inadvertent forest fires, like when one California couple's use of blue-tinted fireworks at a gender reveal in 2021 started the El Dorado Fire, which burned close to twenty-three thousand acres. Every time I see a gender reveal run through my social media, I think to myself, "Good luck!"

In our case, our lack of gender reveal prepared us no better. When Rachel was pregnant, we had decided to wait until the birth to find out the sex of the baby. The only vocal opposition to this decision came from my grandmother Gene. As the undisputed matriarch of the family and the self-professed second-oldest Kappa Delta in the state of Alabama at the time, she was a magnolia-scented force of nature, and she felt it was her duty to talk us out of this plan. I caught her at a family gathering at the lake, with Rachel marooned on the porch beside her.

"You must understand that we are all just distraught over this mystery," her Southern accent, which elongates the syllables with both eloquence and grace, blocks attempts to interject by replacing the natural pauses in a sentence. If she weren't sipping her drink regularly, she could monologue as well as a Shakespearean monarch. "Withholding whether the child is a boy or a girl means we can't help you prepare."

"What do you mean prepare?" Rookie mistake by Rachel, feeding the beast.

"Oh, honey," Gene took a long slip. "You are doing the work, but we are all having this baby, because it is a member of our family. More importantly, when you have your first baby, it's our first baby all over again. The new baby smells and sounds, oh, the laughter! Why, it keeps us young! Sure, you'll be doing the heavy lifting of the feeding and the changing and the waking up at all hours. But just as your love for that child lets you stretch beyond your limits, we, too, thrive as new grandparents, new aunts and uncles, and even as new great-grandparents. Why, I would have passed years ago into the family crypt if it weren't for the eternal spring of my eleven great-grandchildren."

"You have fourteen great-grandchildren now, Gene," I said.

"Is it fourteen now? I'm pretty sure it's just eleven."

I went ahead and began naming them all for her, including the one named after her.

"She's my favorite because she has the best name!"

I continued trying to wrest the conversation back, knocking off the last few names on the list. "That's fourteen great-grandchildren," I concluded.

"Well, I believe that I was only counting the ones I like." She turned her attention back to Rachel and leaned in. "You want your first child on that list, right?" She held Rachel's bewildered gaze for a breath, and then tilted her head back and laughed and slid the conversation on to the last book she had enjoyed. But this was only her opening salvo. Months later, facing a terminal cancer diagnosis, she held Rachel's hand and pressed her as much as the Valium would allow.

"Please, Rachel, I need to know. Tell me whether you are having a boy or a girl." She was resting on her couch, and we were visiting for what very well could have been the last time.

"Gene, I would tell you, but I honestly don't know. I asked the doctor not to tell me," Rachel replied.

"Doctors don't know everything." Gene contended. "You can tell me, I promise I won't tell anyone else." She gave a little cough into her tissue, probably for effect. Her cancer was not in the lungs, and though I have no doubt she felt terrible, she loved a little flourish.

Then my wife told her. "Okay, Gene," she said, exhaling. "I'm having a girl."

I was shocked. Rachel is a terrible liar, and she would have immediately been questioned if Gene had caught a whiff of deceit or subterfuge. But Gene just beamed, smiling in a way I hadn't seen in months. She squeezed Rachel's hand. She had been let in on the secret; she was at the center again.

Rachel was so convincing in that moment that I thought for sure the doctor had told her and she hadn't told me. But when I confronted her, she assured me. "I just went with my gut. I feel like I'm having a girl. In fact, I'm pretty sure of it. Plus, Gene's never going to know the difference, right? I figured there was no harm in telling her how I feel."

That may have been her excuse, but the feeling only grew stronger in proportion to her belly. In fact, when the doctors plucked our firstborn from my wife's cesarean slit and announced, "It's a boy!" she shouted back, "Prove it!" But Rachel had it more right than the doctor did that day, and Kate has been proving her right ever since.

"I am a girl in my heart."

So this was both a shock and not a shock. Nothing was broken, no pets had expired under questionable circumstances, no trips to the ER. I almost laughed with relief. Plus, we had been hearing versions of this for years now. When my oldest child imagined her future, it was always as a woman. We usually teased her about it or made it a joke about how even the children knew not to grow up to be like me. But there was an important change here.

Maybe we only thought we were skipping the dramatic gender reveal. Instead, we got to do it six years in. Because it was Rachel's and my job to tell the family about Kate's coming out. At the time, almost all my family lived in Alabama. We were a tight-knit group, together most every weekend at the lake with frequent visits with cousins, half-cousins, grandparents, aunts and uncles. We'd show up to swim off a cousin's dock, and Kate would ask as we pulled up, "They know about me, right?," and I'd have to say, "Yes, I've told them," or "No, but I'll tell them while we are here." Both of those

Memorabilia

answers were okay with her, but she was unwilling to stick around if I tried to put the conversation off. To a person, our family took Kate's gender journey in stride. Even my father, who once served as a Republican district attorney for Montgomery and was more than a little country, rolled with both the initial conversation of "Here's what's going on" and the firmer alterations, like name changes and birth certificate modifications.

The family being as supportive as possible was an absolute blessing, but it came with a surprise realization. As I talked to my parents and my brothers and my aunts and uncles and cousins, not one of them pushed back hard about what we were experiencing and what we were doing. All that wonderful support meant that Rachel and I felt no brakes, no tug from a trusted family member urging caution. So when we felt scared or worried or wanted this journey to slow down because it was moving too fast for us, we could not blame it on anyone else. It felt like a roller coaster's slow, unrelenting climb toward the inevitable drop.

Rachel told her parents that fall, and they, too, were extremely supportive of us. Rachel's father was a world-renowned obstetrician out of Jackson, Mississippi, and he dove into the medical research to prepare for our next visit. At their home, after the kids were in bed, we sat in the formal living room for the nightly debrief. This was part of the visitation ritual with their family. After family duties like cooking dinner, reading to the kids, and doing the dishes, the adults sit and converse. Their whole house was museum-quality neat, clean, and organized. The room in which the nightly talks took place was immaculate, decorated in greens and purples. Our place was on the couch, facing the floor-to-ceiling windows, and Rachel's parents sat in their armchairs beside the gas log fireplace. This routine was as comfortable as the last turns on the drive home, but this time I dreaded it. Jim, Rachel's dad, took the clinical approach. He talked through the best studies on gender dysphoria, transgender youth, and medical concerns moving forward. Then he recounted the times he and his fellows had made declarations about a newborn's sex and gender when the children they delivered presented as something less than definitive.

"Wait." I stopped him, snapping out of a half-listening lull. "What do you mean?"

"Well, it's not unheard of for children to be born with underdeveloped genitalia. When the delivering doctor looks for a penis or a vagina, and they see something that doesn't look quite like either totally, they often advise that the baby have what's called a vaginoplasty."

There was a lot to unpack there. "Like, how common is this practice, exactly?"

"Well, the most reliable research I've seen points to between one and two percent[*] of newborns are intersex. That's an umbrella

---

[*] This number is contested in the research now, though organizations supporting the rights of intersex individuals like the United Nations' Office of the High Commissioner for Human Rights and the Center for American Progress still use the 1–2 percent findings. The 1–2 percent number includes a broader swath of individuals than those that identify as intersex culturally and socially. For instance, a person with Turner's syndrome would have been

term for any number of chromosomal or developmental issues that can create abnormal reproductive organs."

"That's a lot of babies," I said.

"It's more common than redheaded children," he said. "Twins are only slightly more common, at three percent of babies."

We have several redheads on my side of the family, and twins as well. "So, intersex means that the child could have biological or physical markers for both female and male. But if the doctor thinks the baby is intersex, they declare a sex anyway?"

"It sounds awful now, but the prevailing practice when presented with a newborn without clear genitalia is to immediately construct it."

"Construct their sex," I said, repeating it to myself to try to understand. Of course. Because not only do we socially construct sex and conflate it with gender but we need evidence to justify those decisions. If 1 to 2 percent of children being born physically discount the sex binary of people being either (and only) male or female and recognizable by their private parts, then we are totally cool with surgery for infants to make them look more normal.

"And we work with what we have, but the doctors are making those determinations based on limited knowledge, time, and experience, and they basically try to construct what they can. The

---

included in early research but may not identify as intersex despite sharing the chromosomal irregularities that typically defines intersex in medical literature. Research that attempts to classify intersex more narrowly puts the number at closer to .018 percent of newborns.

saying in those operating rooms goes 'It's easier to dig a hole than to build a pole.' Nine times out of ten, we reconstruct what's there into a vagina and declare those children 'girls.'"

"And then what? I mean, the story for almost all of us is that if we are born with a penis, we are a boy, and if we are born with a vagina, we are a girl. But if hundreds of babies a year have their organs changed after birth and then are told they are one or the other sex to correspond with the change, not only does that poke a gaping hole in the 'genitals make the sex/gender' argument but also could possibly lead to a lot of kids whose gender and sex don't feel aligned, right?"

"Sim, American medicine is frustratingly compartmentalized. I deliver the babies, make sure Mom is healthy, and then pass them off and never see them again. Until another medical professional comes to us and says, 'I'm treating the long-term harm of your practices,' we have a very limited scope of understanding."

"My child is not intersex, I don't think," I said. I could dwell in this conversation, highlighting the real problems these decisions create, but it would move me away from our particular situation. "But I'm still not sure where we are." Up until this point, Rachel and I had been very careful not to use our own labels for what our child was articulating. We talked about the possibility of Kate being transgender, but we'd withheld using that label around the kid. At this point, there were two reasons in my head for this decision. First, I knew enough to know that gender-illumination journeys are complex and personal. Knowing that nonbinary, gender-fluid, and transgender identities all occupy a nebulous space heavily shaded by an individual's feelings of authenticity, I wanted to be careful not to label my child incorrectly again. But underneath that fine academic excuse was the fact that I was not ready for the reality of a child who lacked the privileges, the automatic social acceptance, that comes with being cisgender. Luckily for me, my family gave me no choice. Unbeknownst to me, my sweet mother-in-law, Gloria, had reacted to our news in her own professional way. Upon hearing of Kate's gender dysphoria, she had gone to the local bookstore and bought texts for herself, us, and the kids. For the kids, she selected *I Am Jazz*, the children's book by Jazz Jennings, one of the few prominent and famous transgender people in America at the time. The book is written for children and chronicles Jazz's own coming out with crayonlike illustrations. So, while I was about to break down in front of my in-laws thinking about how my child is going to function in America's health care system, Kate came bolting into the room. She had her pajamas on and had clearly snuck out of bed to look for reading material. Finding the *I Am Jazz* book within the other grandparent classics had sent her tearing from bed and in among the adults, with no fear of breaking the rules. With the book open and her finger jabbing at a passage, she yelled, "This! This right here! This is me! What is this word?!" The word she could not read but volcanically identified with was "transgender."

Rachel must have felt it, too, because she treated this exchange carefully. She coaxed, "Okay, can you tell us more? What does that mean?"

"I mean, I have a boy body," Kate said, while spreading out her hands out, palms toward us, like she was referencing all of herself, "but I am a girl in my mind."

That's when it struck me. My child was using the present tense. This was a *now* issue. Right at that very moment, my child was telling me something very important and painstakingly considered. I needed to do the same.

As the circle of people in the know expands, it eventually involves communities, people who both know you well and not so much. At the time, our closest community was our church. Rachel was raised in a Historic Baptist church in Jackson, Mississippi, called Northminster Baptist Church. Calling Northminster *Historic* is an attempt to place it in within the theological economy of Christianity in the United States. Southern Baptists drive both the cultural and political culture of the denomination in the United States but often face fierce external and internal criticisms and resistance because of their formalized power brokering. For instance, in 2023, the main Southern Baptist conference voted to formally exclude women from leadership positions within member churches. On the other end of the theological spectrum, Historic Baptists differentiate themselves from Southern Baptists by adhering to the core Baptist belief that everyone, from every background and education level and theological expertise, has a relationship with Jesus and God, and the power within the church structure ought to reflect and honor those relationships. Thus, Historic Baptists often have fairly progressive social views when it comes to race, sexuality, and gender diversity in church leadership and membership in comparison with other Baptist traditions.

Like my wife, I grew up in a church and around church folks, though my church community was a touch more conservative. I was a United Methodist member for much of my childhood, though attendance was not regular or especially communal. I never understood the dogma of church as a kid, and it felt overly ornamental and abstract. Church was fine and all, but it had no bearing or coupling point beyond the worship hall. If lessons in the practical application of religion to our lives were being taught, I missed them. Thus, I spent a bunch of time at church, but it was no more time than was required by my parents. Despite a lack of church allegiance, I grew up ardently Christian, mostly from the influence of the summer camp I attended. Tucked into the Blue Ridge Mountains of western North Carolina, I found an amazing community of Christians of all stripes who had boiled down the lessons of the Bible to pieces I understood: God wants you to be good to one another. That lesson was easily applicable in that environment, running through the woods, swimming in the lake, or playing huge group games on the fields. Kids being kind to kids, particularly when you are away from your family, is a natural fit, and it was heavily reinforced by the adults there. If it weren't for summer camp, which I attended for fifteen years as a camper and later a staffer, I would have drifted from Christianity much sooner.

My experience at that summer camp shaped how I understand religion today, especially when it comes to the use of so-called Christian beliefs to criticize the authentic nature of transgender identity and how to handle transgender individuals. It always felt to me that the most important lesson Jesus passed along was to love everyone, especially those who are isolated, stigmatized, assaulted, or pushed to the borders of society. In essence, make community with those who have none and need it. Transgender folks, and many other shunned by the most powerful organized religions in America, should be prime candidates for that outpouring of love, right? And not a love that says "I'll accept you if you change," but a love that says "God made you unique and amazing, and I love you the way you are."

Which brings me to the other puzzling element of the rejection of transgender folks by conservative Christians. Christianity is a religion of miracles, fueled by the power of God, and those acts often exceed human understanding. The creation of the cosmos, the Immaculate Conception, and walking on water are just some of the examples of the creativity, diversity, and power of God's creations. In all the various and magnificent ways that God created, is it really hard to believe that God would create similar dynamic diversity in humans too? Wouldn't a person who is transgender fit directly into the portfolio of unique and amazing works of God? But conservative Christians are quick to point out that the Bible says God created a man and a woman, and then assume that Adam and Eve were both exactly as they picture them to be and that God never intended their descendants to be anything more than what they believed the originals were. To me though, it seems every time the people in the Bible were like, no, God, these are the finite and binary rules, God says, "Hold my beer." Then the dead rise, the water turns to wine, and the giants fall. When we attempt to limit the abilities of God to the creation of one man and one woman who are exactly as we are and only as we are, we limit God to only what we have experienced, not to what God can do.

These days, I find organized religion more fascinating than spiritually powerful. My requirements for church membership revolve around open space for dialogue and for the questioning and contextualizing of dogma and people trying to do better by other people. Also, a church community usually produced excellent babysitter prospects. When we moved to Birmingham with a one-year-old and a three-year-old, Rachel and I were both eager to find a church community.

After trying a few places in Birmingham, we settled into membership at the Baptist Church of the Covenant in downtown Birmingham. There was much to like about this church. For one thing, it started as a splinter group of First Baptist in Birmingham. In the early 1970s, the preacher there was leading his congregation toward desegregation. The First Baptist church sat in downtown and had both Black and white attendees, but had only white leadership and membership. In the early 1970s, a longtime attendee, who was Black, attempted to join the all-white membership. With what seemed like a friendly and welcoming congregation, and with the support of the pastor, the application for membership should have been a breeze. But word spread, and on the day of the presentation of new members, the church was packed with riled-up white members, some of whom hadn't attended in years. Hopes of membership for all the families that day quickly faded. Baptists vote on everything within the church, from how the budget is spent to who is allowed to join, and this vote went against the prospective Black members. In protest, the pastor and about a third of the church walked out and started Baptist Church of the Covenant with the traditional Baptist mission and messaging that "all are welcome." By the time we joined the church, it seemed to be continuing to strive for acceptance, love, and community engagement. The congregation was racially diverse, both the pastor and the associate pastor were women, and there were several queer folks serving at different levels of church leadership, including as deacons.

Most importantly, they seemed perfectly willing to put up with me. I'm typically mistrustful of people who claim they have a higher understanding, who are overtly righteous or evangelical, or who ask faith to replace logic, reason, and lived experience. I'm not atheist or agnostic, but my bullshit meter is on high alert in regard to organized religion, and I just can't stand it when religious teachings don't match up with practice in real life. I don't need God or a religious text to tell me that I should be kind to people, but if you claim to be Christian and can't love everybody the way God made them, we're going to have a hard time getting along. But what I found at the Baptist Church of the Covenant were a lot of people who liked debating the complexities and contradictions that manifest in applying religion to people's lives. There was an excellent pastor named Sarah Shelton, a kind soul who was also a pistol and a firecracker, as my grandmother would have put it. The associate pastor, Valerie, and her husband, Allan, became lifelong

Memorabilia

friends, and the rest of the church leadership was made up of genuinely good people. The preachers pushed us to think, to feel, and to apply those practices to the world around us, and the deacons, who are a leadership body within the church made of members, were radically diverse in age, gender, race, and background. It felt like a wonderful middle ground, a traditional Christian theology with a community-engagement focus that affirmed and accepted the people within their communities. Needless to say, it was the ideal spot for my family to land in 2012. Very quickly, we made friends at church who would become as close as family, and so did our kids. Some of those connections began on Sundays, bleeding over from Saturday college football watch parties, but what really hooked us was a crazy weekend in Panama City Beach, Florida, called Beach Retreat.

Every Labor Day, Baptist Church of the Covenant hosts its Beach Retreat in PCB. The church rents out half of a large Christian retreat center across the road from the Gulf of Mexico. The complex used to be a series of adjacent motels and still sports the layout inside and out with distinctly hourly rate–style rooms crammed with extra bunks that open to grassy courtyards with small pools. Each old motel area also comes with a large industrial kitchen and eating area, so the complex can host several groups simultaneously without too much overlap. Most importantly, the complex sits directly across the street from the Gulf Coast beach. Even loaded down with beach gear and lotioned toddlers, all you had to do was cross the sleepy beach road and walk a short boardwalk to reach the fine white sand and warm water.

For the church, Beach Retreat started as a youth-centered retreat, with a small handful of high schoolers enjoying a long weekend away from their parents. But when the number of chaperones far exceeded the number of youths attending, it became clear to church leadership that a multigenerational retreat was just what their community needed. Thus, Beach Retreat was opened to the congregation, and families of all types, along with a good handful of singles, leap at the chance every year to sleep in crappy bunk beds and use old motel-style bathrooms. Everyone, from the most affluent to the least, comes on the trip. Some folks pay out the nose to rent ritzier digs down the road but spend the day at the complex. Others ride the five-plus hours on the church bus because they have no reliable transportation. The church discounts the expenses for many community members with limited means, making Beach Retreat the only yearly vacation for many church members and their families. Other members bring extended family who have never attended BCOC or even lived out of town. Some churches have members you only see at Easter and Christmas services. BCOC has members who only show up for Beach Retreat.

In the years we attended, from 2012 to 2018, BCOC rented nearly the entire complex, squeezing hundreds of churchgoers into every space available. No one's room was nice, but there was enough variety in layout, size, and amenity that rooming requests were frequently made and ignored. The "best" rooms, like the ones with TV screens bigger than thirty-five inches, more than one shower, or a bedroom with a door that separated it from the bunks, went to multiple families who were willing to stay together. We regularly stayed with other families in order to have access to a full-size fridge or a bathtub. After that, the housing philosophy was "you get what you get, and you don't pitch a fit." Programming was similarly sparse, with a simple sunset Sunday service on the beach and limited midday activities in the few air-conditioned spaces, buffered by the easiest-to-make low-cost meals we could get away with. But no one came for the rooms, the food, or the programming. It was PCB! Kids of all ages, parents, singles, and couples spent time in the sun, moving back and forth between the group of folks on the beach and the parties in the courtyard pools.

At night, most people moved off the beach and found either a circle of lawn chairs in the courtyard or a football game in someone's room to watch. And while alcohol is strictly prohibited by the overtly Christian retreat center that operated the complex, drinking was only frowned upon by our church leadership. Thus, a Prohibition-style drinking culture emerged. Several rooms functioned almost like speakeasies, where Yeti cups were filled discreetly but generously as folks made the rounds from group to group. Church leadership balanced their roles and their hobbies with more discretion. The first year I went to Beach Retreat, the pastor pulled me aside and said, "The Alabama game kicks off at two thirty. I'm going to watch up in my room, and you're welcome to join me, but don't tell anybody. I like to curse during the games, but that's not for everybody in our congregation." I knew we had landed in a good spot.

Because of the layout of the retreat and the intentionally

communal nature of the weekend and activities, Beach Retreat was also the place where everyone spent the weekend catching up with everybody else. From the layout and assignment of the rooms to the meals to the activities, the weekend was designed for fellowship. Every night, people would mingle and mix and catch up with folks they had seen only briefly on Sundays, and children played in ever-morphing bunches, blending with different ages and cliques. This was especially nice for the parents, because communal parenting rules were in full effect. Many times, an adult or two would stay at the pool and be in de facto charge of whatever kid gang showed up. It made the combination of attempting to vacation and parent a whole lot more enjoyable, but it definitely complicated our situation in the summer of social transition.

"I am a girl in my heart." And then, when pressed, "I have a boy body, but I am a girl in my mind." It was present tense, "I am" and "I have," not the "I will be" or the "someday" we had become accustomed to. It finally cracked my heart that she was coming out.

Beach Retreat hit the calendar a cool two months after the "I'm a girl in my heart and mind" conversation. To this point, we had talked to family and a small set of friends, but our bubble was very small. What's more, Kate was only beginning to bend gender norms to fit how she felt. Early on, long before name changes and pronoun adjustments, my eldest would express femininity outwardly solely through clothing. When allowed, dresses were worn in the house nonstop. For the end of the summer, Kate had begun to tentatively wear dresses outside the house as well. She was very careful to ask exactly where we were going, how long we would be there, and who we might see. If she trusted the people in the space, she would wear a dress then too. She started very conservatively. As she grew more comfortable, the combination of her short hair and wearing dresses to places like the grocery store would earn double takes and side-eyed glances from strangers, but that was all. The danger I could foresee coming was bathing suits. It was summer in Alabama, and we vacationed at the lake house nearly every weekend, and during the time we were in town, we often met friends at the community pool. Our kids practically lived in bathing suits up until that point, and suddenly I was doing everything I could to keep us away from bodies of water. So where did my oldest child decide to debut her first public girl's bathing suit? The 2014 Baptist Church of the Covenant Beach Retreat.

Kate had told us that she wanted to bring a girl's bathing suit to Beach Retreat, and it had made it into our luggage after several "Are you sure?" conversations. Many of our closest friends from church were in the loop, but, to our knowledge, Kate had not told any of her friends yet, and the Beach Retreat crowd far surpassed our small bubble. Our oldest suddenly sporting a girl's bathing suit was going to generate a lot of unavoidable conversations, among both the kids and the adults. That meant that all that communal hangout time, from sitting on the beach and by the pool to hanging out in the courtyards, to even the giant community meals, was going to involve me having to work every curious adult through my kid's coming out. As comfortable as I felt at BCOC, I dreaded a weekend of filling in everyone loosely affiliated with the church about our current family situation.

After a Friday and a Saturday of board shorts and a long-sleeve rash guard, Kate broke out her fringy, green-skirted one-piece suit on Sunday. Swimming with her sister and her friend Molly, whose parents had prepped her, everything was going great until the crew of boys Kate's age came through the fence to join the kids at the pool. They stopped at the pool's edge, heads tilted to the side, trying to process what they saw. In the front, and especially slack-jawed, was Marshall, the associate pastor's son. "Are you wearing a girl's bathing suit?" he asked.

"Yeah," she said offhandedly, barely looking up from her pool noodle as she tried to blow water on her sister, Evelyn.

"So are you a girl now?" another kid in the group called.

"Yeah," she repeated, but stopped playing and looked right at the boys. I remember it was painfully bright by the poolside. It was too much sun, and we were too exposed. The sun reflected off the water under and through my glasses, and the parts of my eyes the sun wasn't burning, the chlorine was attacking. I'm seeing this pivotal coming out unfold as casually and delicately as a flower blooms, and I can do nothing but watch.

"Can we play Marco Polo with y'all?" Marshall asked.

"Sure!" And that was that. They played together in the pool for hours, falling right back into their patterns of play, laughing and splashing and wearing themselves into that still hum of exhaustion, where there was nothing left to do but sit by the poolside, bare feet dangling in the water, and eat ice cream so messily that they have an excuse to slip back in the water and go again. The children of Baptist Church of the Covenant welcomed Kate. To this day, her best friends are from that church. BCOC went far beyond tolerance, and the love was palpable.

Not long after Kate came out publicly to the church in that pool in PCB, the women's knitting group at the church surprised us with a new pink baby blanket. Typically reserved for newborns in the church, Kate's blanket was a public gesture of support, love, and excitement for her and us, as parents. I cannot think of a more touching way they could have welcomed her rebirth in the church.

> Later that night, my wife and I debriefed. What had we said after "I am a girl in my mind"? Had we been loving and supportive? We thought so, and Kate went away seeming satisfied and placated. But what's next? Well, the first question that plagued us was, did we believe this? And I wish I could say that it was centered in the concept that our young child could know herself well enough to articulate this giant thing. That she is transgender, a word she had not used, but we knew. But it was probably less about what Kate knew about herself at that moment and more about our terror that she might be right.

When people hear that Kate was not quite seven years old when she came out as transgender, there is often a beat in the conversation while people let it sink in what that might entail. I'm talking about a child who is in between kindergarten and first grade. How does a six-year-old articulate gender dysphoria, gender binaries, or the complexities of gender expression when they are still grasping reading and how to ties shoes? These are legitimate questions, ones I've wrestled with myself. Can a six-year-old actually come out as transgender? And I get that. The answer is: All they can do is try. Their parents, their friends, and the other people in their lives must step up and help them.

It finally became clear to me after Beach Retreat that I was terrified of what my daughter was trying to tell me. I was being supportive, but I wasn't being brave. Kate showed me over and over again what bravery looked like. I had been focused on my emotions, because those did need tending since none of this works unless you deal with how you feel. Your emotions steer the ship. When a parent finds themselves here, their feelings are the life jacket that keeps them afloat or the stone that sinks them. But being afraid was not the place to stop; it was the place to begin. If I wanted to be the best father I could be to Kate, I was going to have to get a lot braver.

The other important question is the one that threw me so many years ago as I sat on that panel. If I could give advice to parents, it's to work your way through your feelings in those coming-out moments. Label what you are feeling and figure out why you have that feeling in this context. I was afraid because I knew that being trans would make my child's life harder. I was ashamed because I did not know what to do. I was sad because I knew her life would not be like mine had been. All of those feelings came from a place of love.

Because I love my child, I can support her even when I am afraid for her, ashamed of myself, and grieving the loss of the easy life I had hoped she would have. The good news is that you'll get lots of practice. I thought coming out was a one-off, like once that cat was out of the bag, it was said and done. But it doesn't work like that. Coming out is not a single moment but thousands and thousands of moments, big and small, when a person reveals a sacred truth about themselves to others. Situations where we expose ourselves so vulnerably are always anxious moments, and those are compounded by each person's fears, beliefs, and expectations. But each time you are there for that process, you have a chance to do it better than you did the time before. I'm lucky that my daughter Kate led me through the tough spots, where my fear overshadowed my expression of love and support for her. I hope that someday she'll say she was lucky to have me for the same reasons.

3
Playing Pretend

From the first month after her seventh birthday, Kate was out to her family, her friends, and much of our wider community. This means I started getting lots of questions—many supportive, many curious, and a few baked in righteous judgment. I've had a lot of practice answering these questions both for myself and for other people. Some questions are quite easy; others involve a lot of context and backstory. Some linger in my brain. But if you would ask me the hardest question I faced, it was whether Kate's feelings and identity expression could just be a phase. And I hear this sentiment echoed when I talk to other parents of trans kids, from well-intentioned and curious family and friends and from critics who believe that there is no such thing as a transgender identity, only a confused cisgender person. "Is it just a phase?" This question comes to my mind regularly because to say it is just a phase is the easiest and safest way for my daughter to avoid the stigmatization and danger she might face as she grows older. The possibility of my daughter's gender dysphoria melting away the same way a young cisgender woman's tomboy time might leave her as she matures affects how I handle Kate's current discomfort with who she is and how she presents to the world as well as the future ramifications of her being transgender in a potentially hostile world.

But that's not usually the question that people start with. Before that question gets launched, people usually work up to it by trying to understand the context of what they're seeing. So when we first told people that Kate was socially transitioning, a lot of people wanted to know what exactly that meant.

Question #1: What do you mean by "social transition"?

In doing research with the transgender, nonbinary, and gender-diverse community, it is clear to me that *transitioning* means lots of different things. As I understand it, in the broadest strokes, transitioning reflects a realignment of gender (a sense of masculinity and/or femininity, manliness and/or womanliness) identity (the internal feelings of who one is) with the presentation of gender to the outside world, called *gender expression*. Society has lots of rules, spoken and unspoken, about what boys should be like and what girls should be like. These rarely fit well for everyone, even cisgender folks, but they especially don't fit for anyone who doesn't identify as cisgender. But once you leave the broadest strokes, transition can look drastically different from one person to another based on everything from available means and health care to personal goals. Even in the transgender community, every adult's journey to living a life that matches who they are on the inside is unique. Adults have options (though limited and strictly guarded) as to how to transition socially, legally, and physically. Sometimes, the transition for a transgender person involves gender-affirming surgery, in which genitalia is reshaped so that sex and sexual organs match the gender identity. Often, people forgo surgery and keep the bodies they have. Sometimes, transitioning means using hormone blockers to stall or stop puberty. And sometimes, transitioning means altering pronouns. Sometimes, legal issues arise, like those related to name changes and gender markers on passports. Other times, it may be that the person feels that they have transitioned when they wear clothing that better expresses who they are.

For children, the process is simple and totally reversible. When a child as young as Kate (about to turn seven) vehemently connects with a transgender identity, there are no physical medical interventions. In our case, our medical team, including Kate's pediatrician, her mental health counselor, Rachel's and my mental health counselor, and others, advised us to let Kate express her femininity through socially transitioning. Under the guidance of several mental health professionals and her pediatrician, and following the best practice guidelines of the American Medical Association, the American College of Pediatrics, and the American Psychological Association, we let Kate begin presenting as a little girl. As I discussed earlier, one important aspect of her social transition was wearing dresses and girls' bathing suits. This quickly went from an every-now-and-then occurrence to an everyday thing because of the way she felt as a result. The other key expression for Kate was her hair. Having had short hair her whole life, she wanted to grow her hair out as long as possible. Long hair shifts a stranger's first gender guess from boy to girl. She loves having long hair, though she rarely combs it.

Also, pretty early in this process, we switched to calling her Kate and using she/her/hers pronouns. We did not legally change her name until years later, but that did not matter to her nearly as much as being called Kate mattered. And that's one of the most important parts of the social transition stage: Nothing is permanent. If Kate had hit a point during this period where she thought, "Wait a minute, this doesn't feel right," then she could have just cut her hair short again and stopped wearing dresses. The impermanence of the social transition period also smoothed the way for many of our friends, family, and acquaintances. Plus, all the research said that the only permanent damage that could be done at this point was through denying the child's feelings and expressions of self.

The malleability of the social transition period also has its downside. Because nothing feels set yet, the idea that everything will go back to "normal" is enticing, even for the most supportive parents. Let me clarify: I believe there is nothing abnormal about being transgender. But every parent tries to anticipate the struggles their children will face and to prepare them for those struggles, and most of what we anticipate is based on our own lived experiences. So if a great struggle of my young life was being the shortest kid in my class until eleventh grade, then I conceptualize that as a "normal" struggle, even when I objectively know it was not routine or common. It was unique to me, as no one else in my class had to deal with that, because when you are the shortest kid in the class, everyone else has at least one person they are taller than. This same logical break functions for me as the parent of a trans kid, but it is magnified by the real dangers trans folks face. I myself succeeded in overcoming being shorter than my peers, and so I have confidence I could help my children through those, admittingly minor, hurdles. On the other hand, I have no personal experience with gender dysphoria or identifying with a gender that doesn't match my sex. And I'm smart enough to know that being temporarily tiny is nothing compared with the social stigmatization, violence, and isolation that many transgender people face.

Question #2: How do you know that social transition is a good option?

Thinking about reintroducing your child to your family and friends, and that neighbor you barely know, with a new name and sporting a dress when they have only ever known your child as a boy is a little daunting. But I'd wager that every parent has had kids do things that buck gender norms at some point. Maybe that masculine little boy who loves his G.I. Joes has been stealing his sister's Barbies during playtime, and not just so the Joes have love interests. Or you've got a daughter who is damn good at throwing a football. When I was a kid, my older cousins would dress me up for their tea parties, and the pictures are still circulated every now and then at Thanksgiving. Does that mean I'm harboring a secret trans identity too? Of course not. But it does highlight that our social constructions of gender and the norms that go with it are rigid and tightly enforced, particularly by adults. Passing around the picture of me in drag is not to celebrate my gender fluidity or my comfort with my masculinity, but to laugh at me. The point is that even the most cisgender kids' play doesn't always fit well in our social norms of gender because there are major problems with our social norms, not with the kid. So after I explain what social transition is, I usually get some form of a question about when you feel confident embracing the social transition. For us, Kate's articulation of her trans status followed a well-worn three-word phrase that was passed around a lot in our family groups: insistent, consistent, and persistent. While not the case for everyone every time, this three-word mantra is a measuring tool for assessing a child's gender dysphoria. When the child claims a gender different from the one assigned at birth, are they insistent? When they express their gender as something different from the gender assigned at birth, are they consistent in that expression? When the child is corrected, do they persist in their expression of who they truly are? And once Rachel and I started adding up the evidence, these were pretty easy to answer. Kate had been talking about being a girl or growing up to be a woman for years. She used contextual cues as well as language, like always dressing up as a girl during play, whether it was a princess or a cowgirl. And her reactions to pushback were volcanic. Using these informal guidelines, we could confidently say that Kate's language and actions fit those three markers. And sure, I just gave examples that show that all kids at least flirt with, if not openly challenge, our social norms around gender. But nine times out of ten, they encounter pushback in some form or fashion and fold back into the norms. Questions of insistence, consistence, and persistence help you examine the depth of a child's commitment in the face of pushback.

Question #3: So you are having these conversations regularly?

The measuring stick of "insistent, consistent, and persistent" is great and all, but it gives the impression that every night at dinner we discuss the complexities of gender expression, probing and analyzing the child's every thought while they are captive in their highchairs. Then we tally the gender expressions in a spreadsheet, and if the old abacus leans one way, we have a definitive answer. I mean, yes, a researcher can create guidelines that work great in a laboratory setting or in a controlled study, but anyone who has raised kids knows that it's 90 percent chaos and 10 percent desperation naps. Plus, even when a kid is expressing gender, they aren't doing it in scientific terms. Hell, they aren't even doing it with adult language. Even still, the signs add up.

When Kate was very young, like four and five, and would get in trouble, we would put her on leotard restriction. This is not some parent code speak or pediatric psychology euphemism; it was exactly as it sounds. When Kate would do something she knew she wasn't supposed to do and there needed to be consequences, we took away her leotards. We actually stumbled upon this punishment out of desperation. Before we started socially transitioning, Kate got in trouble often. Not only was she impulse-driven, like all young children, but she also seemed to lack any sense of self-preservation. She's the first to try a homemade zip line, sled down a steep slope, or climb a tree to the top. In the first tree house I built for the kids, I put in a slide. Once completed, the consensus from the adults was that it was pretty high and steep for the kids (then two and three). But that didn't stop Kate from chucking herself down it over and over again.

To make matters worse, she grew to be clever and calculating and was always up to something. Worst of all, or best of all if it isn't your job to try to keep her alive, she revels in her creative solutions to getting around the rules. Let me give you an example: One time, when she was six and her sister, Evelyn, was five, they were playing hide-and-seek while I cooked dinner. Evelyn had just gotten the best of Kate by moving some pots and pans aside and hiding in the kitchen cabinet. Not to be one-upped, my oldest thought she'd raise the stakes. She patiently waited to hide until I had left the kitchen to get some gumbo from the chest freezer in the garage. When I came back, I opened the refrigerator, and she came tumbling out. Luckily, she had closed herself in only for a moment and was not injured in the incident. But when I tried to express to her how dangerous such a hiding place was, she simply smiled at her sister and said, "Yeah, but she never would've found me!"

On top of being devious and having a total disregard for safety, Kate also has the ability to entertain herself with her imagination. This makes any type of time-out-style consequence more of a reward than a punishment. Oftentimes, she relished taking a book and reading in her room or making up an adventure story while sitting in time-out. Nothing frustrated my wife more than trying to squeeze self-reflection, regret, or boredom from this wonderfully creative child who is happiest in her isolation. She once came to the end of a significantly long nose-in-the-corner session and immediately said, "Mommy, listen to the song I made up" and happily sang her a rhyming three-verse song. It was a funny song, and my wife cried, totally beaten.

The real issue was that she was always doing something that got her in trouble. Up until the time that she was able to articulate her gender dysphoria, my oldest child acted out in several very disconcerting ways. For instance, she would lie extravagantly any time she wanted to get out of a situation. I once dropped by her school unexpectedly and found her not in her kindergarten classroom but sitting at the receptionist desk coloring a picture. When I asked the administrator sitting next to her what was going on, she told me, "Oh, she's just a little extra sad because her mom is out of town."

"Rachel isn't out of town," I said, looking directly at Kate. "She's at the grocery store, but she's in town."

Kate pretended to ignore the exchange, watching side-eyed as discreetly as possible, but she never stopped coloring. The school administrator was at a loss for words and looked at Kate slack-jawed for several seconds as Kate avoided eye contact. Eventually, the administrator said, "Maybe you should go back to class," and Kate smoothly slipped out of the office.

Then we had this whole phase of stealing, mostly from friends. We'd find trinkets we had never purchased, like a Big Ben souvenir key chain and a micro-machine-style car, in the pockets of her clothes or stuffed in her backpack or lunchbox. When confronted, she'd often confess that she had nicked the item so long ago she couldn't remember who it actually belonged to. Needless to say, she stayed in trouble.

So we had this combination of a clever and devious child who was acting out all the time and who was totally impervious to time-out. And naturally, desperate times call for desperate measures, and leotard restriction was born. We settled on leotards because they were her favorite thing to wear. Keep in mind, at this point in my child's life, five and six years old, everyone thought of her as a little boy. She had short blond hair, answered to a boy's name, and wore seersucker shorts and polo shirts to school like they were designed for her. But when she got home from school every day, and all weekend, she would play dress-up. She liked to dress up so much that we would go and buy all the leftover costumes on sale at department stores after Halloween and give them to her for Christmas. But when she dressed up, she almost exclusively dressed up in feminine clothes. She would dress like a princess, complete with a wig, or a cowgirl with a pink frilly skirt, or a ballerina, and, more often than not, she would be sporting a leotard. As parents, we thought it was great. Our child was wonderfully imaginative, and we didn't think it was a big deal that she admired female heroines, princesses, and superheroes. But what resonated with us was the consistency and the ferocity with which she used her dress-up time to act her feminine presentation. And anyone who mistook the ten-gallon-hat-wearing, boot-stompin', plastic-six-gun-slinging six-year-old for a cow*boy* instead of cow*girl* would immediately be corrected with a stern word and a death stare from the child. And if an adult were to insist that gender norms and rules be enacted, she would go to extremes.

The October she was six years old, my mother came to walk her and her younger sister around the neighborhood for Halloween. Kate had chosen to dress up as Batgirl, and the costume included both Batman-branded components and Batgirl-specific flair, as best we could put together. But my mother insisted that Kate was actually Batman. Kate became so frustrated that she took off the costume ten minutes prior to walking out the door to trick-or-treat, found a pair of scissors, and cut the entire costume into three-inch strips so she wouldn't be forced to wear it around the neighborhood.

Question #4: Could she just be pretending?

Even as kids, we understand the difference between pretending to be something and being something. Let me give you an example. When I was a kid, the best birthday party you could have in Montgomery, Alabama, was going to Looney's Skating Rink across from the Montgomery Mall. There wasn't anything particularly impressive about the skating rink. It felt like nothing had changed since it was built sometime in the mid-1960s. There was still shag carpet that looked like it had been collecting spilled Cherry Coke and spat-out Juicy Fruit gum for decades, brown leather skates with orange wheels that seemed to weigh thirty pounds each, and a disco ball in the middle of the painted concrete oval floor. But what Looney's was missing in up-to-date furnishings and cleanliness, it more than made up for in its birthday party programming. There was a free skate, of course, followed by coordinated (not describing the skaters here) dance routines, including the Hokey-Pokey and the Electric Slide, and several competitions that always seemed to level out the athleticism gaps often faced in elementary and middle school. And always, there was some sort of special game, attention, or duty bestowed upon the birthday boy or girl. I must have attended dozens and dozens of nearly identical Looney's Skating Rink birthday parties growing up, and when I turned nine years old, I finally got my own. My two best friends at the time were Richard Kohn and Thomas Oliver. Besides our friendship, there was no logical reason to celebrate our birthdays together. Richard's birthday was in January, Thomas was a September kid, and mine was two days before Christmas. Nevertheless, our parents somehow decided that a birthday together on some random weekend was better than three birthdays apart. The invitations were a homemade special. A headshot photo of each of us was displayed prominently on a Wanted poster, with invitation information peppered with language stripped from the FBI's Most Wanted list: "Interested posse members should meet at Looney's Skating Rink on September 9" and "Be on the lookout for three guys armed and skating dangerously." It didn't bother me at the time that a criminal-themed birthday party didn't jibe with Looney's inescapable disco feel. I didn't care about the invitation or my parents' reasoning behind our theme. Adults were weird;

the important thing was Looney's. But when my grandfather, the sheriff, made a surprise visit, the reason for the theme finally dawned on me.

Everyone was gathered around the cutting of the cookie cake, just after singing "Happy Birthday" with our skates still on, when the double doors to Looney's burst open and the sheriff of Montgomery County, with deputies in tow, raided the building. Dressed in full uniform and backlit with flashing blue lights from their cars in the parking lot, my grandfather held up the Wanted Poster invitation and boomed out, "I'm looking for these three boys!"

All hell broke loose. Each of us was mobbed by our so-called friends, dragged over to the deputies to be handcuffed, fingerprinted, and photographed with the deputies. It seemed to happen in slow motion. Richard, stuck at the middle table, had no chance of escape, but Thomas, whose cake was on the end of the table closest to the deputies, nervously backed away from the scene, only to be tackled at the edge of the rink floor. Realizing that I had been tricked into this photo op by my parents, I decided not to go down without a fight. I immediately skirted a few folks who were still trying to grasp what was going on, and made it to the rink floor before anyone could catch me. Then the race was on. Trailed closely by a makeshift posse of sugar-crazed nine-year-olds, I skated away as fast as possible. And while the adrenaline kept me just out of arm's reach for the first thirty seconds, the futility of my escape dawned on me as I reached the end of the rink. The back wall offered no cover or exit, only a balance bar mounted on the concrete wall. Avoiding the wall meant following the rink as it curved to the left, forcing me to turn back toward the chaos. In my desperation, I decided not to turn and instead skated full speed into the back wall, wrapped my arms tightly around the balance bar that served as a barrier from the concrete lawsuit waiting to happen, and dared my friends to drag me back. Fortunately for me, they didn't try very hard. None of them were able to break my grip, and there was cookie cake waiting to be eaten, so few engaged in the exercise for long. The chase was fun, but physically struggling against a determined, wiry, and athletic nine-year-old, not so much. Only a few stragglers were there a few minutes later when my father walked down the rink toward me. "Game on," I thought, and settled in for the struggle.

But when he got to me, he kneeled down, looked me over, and asked, "Are you okay?"

It was like an actor breaking the fourth wall. I was surprised, because I thought we were playing a game of pretend, a ruse initiated by my parents, enlivened by my grandfather, and currently being won by me. Why wouldn't everything be okay?

"I am, yes, sir," I said, sheepishly still gripping the railing.

"You sure?" The question was not intended to prolong the conversation; the flatness of his tone made sure of that. My father was not being patient but was directing me to think about what was going to happen next.

"Yes, sir," I said, trying to hold the railing more nonchalantly.

"Good," my father said, straightening up. "Then come take some pictures and eat some cake. Your grandfather's got shit to do, but he wasn't going to miss your birthday party."

Playing Pretend

Skating slowly back across the rink beside my father, the weirdness of the scene was more apparent. My grandfather loved me, and showed it with his time, his gentleness, and his attention. But it occurs to me that he was not disconnected in these two identities, my grandfather and the sheriff. I had rarely, if ever, seen him messing around in uniform. It was like, he was always my grandfather, but when he was sheriff another, more adult side of his life was visible. I would go to work with him as his helper, and he'd have to balance these two roles. But in this case, he wasn't. He was playing sheriff for me. And I didn't like it. And when I arrived for my turn in handcuffs, I could tell he didn't like it either. He took pictures with each of us but did not laugh or smile. He left without cake.

Part of me thinks that his discomfort centered on the premise of the ruse: He was there to arrest children. I'm sure the parents assumed it would be funny and ridiculous—who gets arrested at their ninth birthday party? None of the organizing parents seemed to consider that this might actually be part of his job as the sheriff. As deputies spread throughout Montgomery County, their daily jobs involved interactions with community members of all ages, and most certainly included children making unlawful decisions. This was the late 1980s, Reagan was still the president, so "Just Say No," the War on Drugs, and zero-tolerance laws recentered America's law-and-order obsession with recreational drug use on young people. U.S. Department of Justice data claim that the juvenile arrest rate during the late 1980s and early 1990s was among the highest in history. The year of my birthday, the Office of Juvenile Justice and Delinquency Prevention reported an arrest rate of 7,336 people seventeen years old and under per 100,000. That number started to decline steadily in the mid-1990s to 1,269 per 100,000 in 2020. To put it another way, the juvenile arrest rate was 478 percent higher during my ninth birthday party than it was at my fortieth birthday. Undoubtedly, those deputies had arrested kids, and not in the pretend way we were experiencing. Wrestling with the magnitude of that authority, putting handcuffs on someone, much less a young person, would be troubling for anyone. In this case, placing the cuffs on your grandson, your namesake, slams the point home. My grandfather was a sucker for children. If a baby was crying in a restaurant, he would comfort it while the parents ate their dinner. I lost count of how many times I watched a complete stranger hand over their child to him so they could finish their meal and how deftly he'd win the child over. Back at our table, the child would give up crying and shift almost magically to giggling with my grandfather and then back to crying when the parents reclaimed them. But here was one of the gentlest men I have ever known, doing something decidedly ungentle while being asked to smile for the picture.

Nor did it seem to occur to anyone that some of these children would indeed be arrested one day. It stands to reason that some of us would face legal trouble at some time in our lives, and possibly face arrest. The reasoning was probably easier to ignore because of our cultural privilege. Almost every kid at the party was white and affluent. For those of us occupying that social space, law enforcement's role is to serve and protect us. Pretending to be arrested, then, was acceptable and laughable because it juxtaposed our social standing with an absurd reality. The fact that children being arrested was an actual reality for many in our town was probably not considered, if I'm being kind, or was altogether ignored for the sake of the joke, if I'm being honest.

I was pretending to be the criminal, but there were limits and consequences to that pretending. There was a clear beginning and an end, one that I had gone past. My grandfather, on the other hand, was still going to be sheriff when he left my party. He might actually have to arrest a kid that day or the next. There are limits to pretending. The things we hold as identity are not phases, because we don't turn them off.

Question #5: Could this just be a phase?

And here we are. Even if people get what social transition is and can differentiate between pretend and genuine and deep feelings, doubts usually linger as to the permanence of this identity. "The kid lived their first six years as a boy, so what if they want to go back again to being a boy in six years?" they either say or think to themselves. That leads to the question "Could your kid be going through a phase?"

Kids go through phases, that's undeniable. But think about all that the question asks of a parent and what it reveals about the asker. I define a phase as strongly held beliefs/interests, behaviors, habits, or attitudes inside a time frame with a clear beginning and end. The ukulele phase, the bowhunting phase, or the Corvette phase of your life is marked by both the intensity with which you obsessed over that thing and the acknowledgment that the fixation was temporary. When someone asks "Could this be a phase?" they are focused on the idea that the child's concept of gender could change in the future, and therein lies the first problem. How does a parent determine whether or not something is a phase while they are living in the middle of it? Of cours, it could be a phase; only time will tell. So, if you can't know whether it's a phase, the response becomes "So what?" So what if it is a phase, I'm still going to listen to my child and support them now and in the future. I'm going to love them vehemently as they work through understanding themselves as a child, a teenager, a young adult, and then, if the good Lord's willing and the creek don't rise, when they are parents of children too.

But more importantly, the question frames the ability to reason through it in the wrong spot. Instead of speculating on whether this is the final place on the gender journey, treat it like a new beginning and see what changes for the better. First, think about a scenario in which a cisgender kid goes through a phase where they challenge gender norms, like a little boy who loves to wear dresses. The harms are limited, and the rewards may be great. I want my cisgender younger daughter to question binary categorical identity systems, because they do more harm than good. Now think about this scenario for a kid who insists they are trans. If a child goes through a phase where they experience gender fluidity and they go by another name and grow their hair out, what lasting harm does it cause them? Sure, there are inherent risks of presenting nonbinary gender expressions in public and some hateful, righteous people out there, but embracing some of your kid's challenges to gender norms seems healthy, particularly in the long term. More likely than not, you'll end up with a child who has a well-developed sense of self, who doesn't harbor deep-seated fears or regrets about how they express gender. But assuming it's *just a phase*, actively attempting to suppress your child's gender expressions comes with dire consequences.

Admittedly, Kate has been through plenty of phases. My favorite was the mermaid phase. She loved those beautiful aquatic women whose fish tails revealed no physical hints of sex. She dressed up like a mermaid, played with mermaids dolls, painted and colored mermaids. We had mermaid tails that the kids could swim in. They were like one big merged set of flippers and, as such, took some getting used to in the pool. But Kate would have rather drowned than take off that tail. Even though the flippers were well constructed, she wore out several pairs long before she outgrew them. Once we took the kids to South Florida on spring break and visited Disney World and, as their favorite April Fool's Day subterfuge ever, went to see the mermaids of Weeki Wachee Springs, an old Florida-style attraction from the 1940s that had been turned into a state park. Weeki Wachee had an alligator show, giant rickety-looking water slides, and kayak trails through their various pools of crystal-clear spring-fed pools. But their defining attraction since the 1940s was their mermaids, who performed various underwater dances and acrobatics while only occasionally taking a pull from kelp-like breathing tubes around the underwater stage.

From the underwater theater, sitting on velvet-upholstered cushions that probably had not been updated since the park opened, I could see Kate loving the mermaid show more than anything we saw in the Magic Kingdom.

But not all her phases were pleasant. She went through the stealing phase, lifting toys and trinkets from friends and classmates. She went through a phase of uncontrollable sadness, where she would burst out sobbing randomly and could not explain why. She went through a phase of self-harm. She would become so frustrated at tiny misfortunes or inconveniences, like, the dog won't come when she called or her shoes became untied, that she would hit herself. Once, I was downstairs and hearing a drumbeat upstairs. Boom, boom, boom. I went to investigate and found Kate banging her head against the wall as hard as she could and crying, not at the pain, but in frustration. She could not (or would not) tell me why she was doing it. This became a regular way for her to process her frustration. If she was close to a wall, she hit it with the side of her head. From that angle, she could not generate much power, and her head would dully thud against the drywall. But when she'd really get stuck, she'd face the wall, plant her palms against the smooth paint, and slam her forehead forward like she was trying to knock herself unconscious. And we could not anticipate what would set her off, so she would get several crushing blows in before we could pull her away and calm her down.

But the worst was when I noticed the knives go missing. I like to cook; I do the majority of the kitchen work, and I like my kitchen organized a specific way. So I noticed when my paring knife disappeared from the block on the kitchen counter. Once I had double-checked the washing stations, the drawers, and the disposal, I headed up to Kate's room, fearful I would find it there. She had tucked it in her sock drawer. I returned it to the block, moved the block to the deepest part of the kitchen counter, and tried to put it out of my mind. A few weeks later, it was gone again. This time, I could not find it in her room, but she had carved runes in her bed's headboard. I interrogated her, pleaded with and threatened her, but got nowhere. The knife never reappeared, and I figured she'd ditched the evidence somewhere outside. The block was moved inside a high cabinet. A month later, a second knife went missing from the block. It was the other small one, a three-inch serrated blade, that had been a neighbor to the first. Again, a search yielded nothing and the interrogation led nowhere. All I could think of was that her self-harm was about to get worse.

Then Kate came out to us, and we began her social transition. Overnight, these nightmarish phases ended as abruptly as they had seemed to start. She stopped stealing, banging her head, or being uncontrollably sad. As her hair grew out, she was as happy as I had ever seen her. She floated instead of trudged. She greeted everyone, smiled, and laughed. The sullen and frustrated child was gone, replaced by the lightest and happiest version of herself. If Kate's transgender identity is a phase, it's the best one she's ever had.

4

Schooling

At some point early in Kate's process of coming out, Rachel and I had to do an assessment of what our plans for her future were and how we could get there. As part of that, we focused in on the seminal experiences of our lives growing up, to try to find a way to replicate some of those experiences. For my wife and me, the three experiences that were central to both of us becoming who we are, as well as we could reckon it, were school, sports, and summer camp. We had several that didn't overlap—I had hunting and fishing, and Rachel had church—so we focused on those three shared areas.

The first we chose to tackle was school, and it's the one where we felt most confident. For one thing, I was a career educator. I got my undergraduate degree from the University of Alabama and stayed for my master's degree in communication studies so I could work with students on the speech and debate team. From there, I taught eighth-grade English and high school speech and debate at a Birmingham college prep school until I was recruited to coach debate at a top-twenty-five liberal arts college in Colorado. Three years of it snowing on Easter had my Mississippi-born wife begging for us to move back to the South. The housing recession meant we still owned a house in Alabama that we couldn't sell before we moved to Colorado, so we moved back. I went and got a PhD and was hired as an assistant professor back at the University of Alabama three years later. I was in my second year on faculty when Kate came out.

Rachel and I had already been extremely intentional about our kids' education as they navigated preschool and kindergarten. When Kate came out in 2015, we had just recently moved into a better school district specifically with the idea that our kids would attend at least the public middle school and high school, though we were pretty happy with the fledgling private Montessori kindergarten and elementary school nearby that both children were attending as pre-K and kindergarten students. Montessori education is project-based learning with an intentional focus on community building as a tool to reinforce lessons. In a Montessori school, classrooms might have first, second, and third graders together, with the older students helping tutor the younger students as a lesson that reinforces the concepts from learning to understanding to mastery. The school where our children started kindergarten was excellent. The teachers were kind, thoughtful, and professional. Our kids liked going to school. The school was also pretty new, only a year or two old when we joined, and as the school grew, we felt like founding community members. We volunteered often, helped with school events, and oriented new families. We were close with teachers and administrators, and they knew we'd help when they asked.

When Kate began her social transition to a girl, she was also about to begin first grade, which meant moving on from the warm glow of kindergarten and entering something that looked and felt like a regular school, with lessons, tests, and projects. Facing both transitions, the gender one and the classroom one, we thought it would be much more disruptive to move the kids to a new school. "We should probably keep them where they are, right?" I said, as we sat on the back deck in one of our many impromptu meetings after the kids were in bed.

"That makes the most sense. The kids are happy there, we're happy with the education they're getting, and the teachers seem to really like the kids," Rachel said.

"Plus, I'm going to be around this year helping them with debate, so if they have any questions or issues, I'll be there." This year, I had volunteered to teach a speech class during the week and to coach a competitive debate team on the weekends to help round out the curriculum and to offer an extracurricular for older students.

"That's fine and all, but you need to promise me you're not going to treat it like a parent-teacher conference."

My parent-teacher conferences are notorious within our family. Part of my problem stems from being a career educator myself, so I have very high standards for what should be happening in the classroom, and I expect the teachers and administrators tasked with educating my child to be able to speak to those standards. On top of that, I cut my teeth in my profession as a speech and debate coach. So, not only do I expect educators to be able to articulate their pedagogical approach, but I also expect them to stand up to hard, albeit well-meaning, questions. Sounds great in principle, but Rachel contends that it feels kind of rough in practice.

All these poor, underpaid, and underappreciated teachers have to be ready to deal with all types of wild-card parents, who might be anywhere on the spectrum from attempting to control every aspect of their child's life to actively ignoring them. I've been there myself and have run my fair share of conferences in which little Billy's parents are wondering how I could ruin a seventh grader's chances at Yale by giving them a B in speech class. I'm scarred enough not to punish a teacher for what a student does (or doesn't do), but I also know that when you take a teacher off script, you learn a lot about what is really happening in the classroom.

At the very first parent-teacher conference I attended as a parent, I embarrassed the hell out of my wife. At the time, the kids attended a national-chain daycare company that billed itself as a pre-kindergarten education program. As such, on top of watching the kids, leading crafts and activities, and overseeing nap time, the teachers of the four- and five-year-olds also had curricular goals to reach with the students. They would ask for a conference with the parents twice a year. At our very first one of these sessions, the teacher had us sitting in those tiny plastic blue chairs while she explained our child's learning style and her pedagogical goals for the year. I thought I was politely listening and asking helpful leading questions. But my questions must've been a little out of the ordinary because the teacher stopped talking to me and addressed only Rachel for most of the meeting. Things really came to a head when the teacher wanted to talk about her concerns.

"I'm growing concerned with your child's work in art class. Here's an example of what has me concerned." From her manila folder she pulled exhibit A: a piece of construction paper with a crayon drawing. She placed the evidence on the table on top of a fine dust of Goldfish leftovers and rotated it for us to view. Written across the top in our child's handwriting was "DOG." Below the title looked like something that come out of an uncovered blender. Scribbles of all different colors emanated from the central space, with some lines dark and straight and then bending at odd angles and others sweeping and thick and twirling. It resembled an explosion of pasta or a tornado hitting a Sherwin-Williams paint factory. But in no conventional way did it resemble a dog.

"Has your child seen a dog before?" the teacher asked us.

I took a quick glance at my clothes, which were covered in dog hair. Between our 110-pound golden retriever and 60-pound yellow lab, our child has known dogs her entire life. But honestly, what kid hasn't seen a dog before? Even kids without dogs are enamored with them. Hell, they have to be one of, if not the most, popular children's story characters. I got the feeling that the teacher was intentionally being ugly, but I held back.

"Yep, she knows what a dog looks like," my wife answers. I turned my head to gauge whether Rachel was seriously participating in this conversation. She didn't strike me as being as concerned as the teacher was. She struck me as someone who was engaging in the conversation so it doesn't last any longer than necessary.

If that was her plan, I blew it sky-high. Sorry, Rachel. "I think it's great," I chimed in. "What's wrong with it?"

"It doesn't look anything like a dog!" She said this in a way that you tell a toddler to take that Cheeto out of their ear. She turned her attention back to Rachel, the reasonable one. "Most of the time," she explained, "when I asked the children to draw a dog, they draw something that at least looks like a dog. They give me a circle with four lines coming down and another circle for the head."

I let that sit for a just a beat. "And that's what a dog looks like to you?" I asked. "A couple circles and four lines? That doesn't sound much like a dog to me."

"Well, no, of course not. But that's what most kids do."

"So when you compare two abstract drawings of dogs, you prefer the one that's most repeated?" I could feel Rachel squirming almost as much as the teacher was, so I tried to give her an out. "Let's talk about the fact that my child wrote 'DOG' on top of the page. Do the other kids know how to spell dog?"

"Well, no. We haven't gotten to the alphabet yet."

"Okay, well, I think I'll trade her lack of conventional artistry for advanced language arts skills." And the meeting was over. Honestly, I thought it went well. Rachel told me I was never allowed to go to another parent-teacher conference.

Knowing I could be a bit much for teachers, Rachel wanted not only to have a proactive approach to Kate's social transition at her school but also to lead the conversation. And that started great. As we marched toward the beginning of the school year, Rachel set up meetings with the administration to alert them and to double-check that there would be no issues. In these meetings, the head of the school came across as sweet, sympathetic, and understanding. When Rachel began our coming-out story from the summer, she reached across the space and took her hand. At the

Schooling

end of the story, she smiled and said, "It sounds like y'all have had quite a summer. Your child is such a sweet person, you know we love *her* here, and she is so lucky to have y'all as parents."

We automatically relaxed. For the next hour and a half, we talked about what was important to us, like calling our child "Kate" instead of her deadname and using feminine pronouns, accessing the girls' restroom, and paying special attention to bullying that could occur. On all these points, we met affirmation and assurances that these would not be issues. The name thing was easy, we were told. The building had only single-user restrooms anyway, she reminded us, so no one should be disturbed or inconvenienced. And she highly doubted that there would be any bullying. "We are such a close-knit community, I can't imagine anyone would bully your child over this. But we can certainly keep our eyes and ears open to the possibility." And we were happy because this was the reaction we expected. We then took the next step to talk to Kate's teacher, a wonderful educator who had split her time between kindergarteners and first graders as they got ready to move up to the first- through third-grade classroom but was slated to be exclusively in the first- through third-grade classroom with Kate that year. She was similarly supportive and kind and already had a wonderful connection with Kate. As the first day of school approached, we thought we were in a great place.

I'm not sure if it was the ease of past experiences with family, friends, and church, but if there were red flags about this school, we totally missed them until it was too late. When we got to school the first day, the kind teacher our child was supposed to have had been reassigned at the last minute to another classroom when a fourth-grade teacher took another job. In her place was a first-time teacher we didn't know. She had landed in town only a month earlier, when the family moved for her husband's new job. When she came to visit the school with her son, who was now attending, she heard about the immediate opening, applied, and was hired in the week.

We walked into the school, met the new teacher, and bolted for the head's office. "Please tell me you prepped her, and Kate's going to be okay in there," I said.

"Yes, of course. It's going to be fine. She's super sweet, and Kate's going to be just fine. You know you have our support," we were assured. With that, we left. We were comforted but not wholly at peace. The problems started almost immediately.

I don't know about you, but I will never forget my first-grade teacher for all the right reasons. Her name was Mrs. Thames, and if she had asked me to jump off a cliff, I would've done so with a smile on my face. I was a clingy child by nature, and Mrs. Thames gave great hugs. She was a thin woman with a beautiful smile and that carefully trimmed 1980s haircut that radiated feminine professionalism for the decade. She exuded gentleness and happiness, and I have no idea if I learned anything in that class other than that Mrs. Thames loved me. And that's what I needed to know: school was a place where I was safe and valued, because only then should I be expected to learn. My daughter didn't get a Mrs. Thames in first grade; she got someone who willfully disregarded her feelings and well-being. She fought us tooth and nail on Kate's name, her gender, and her pronouns and ignored the pain and anguish she caused.

Schooling

Of course, at first we didn't hear about any deviations from our expectations. We didn't hear about it from Kate. Much like me, she very much wants to please others, and so she had not told us about her teacher's insistence on deadnaming her. We put it together by the forms, worksheets, and other materials that made their way home with Kate. Written at the top of each, in the teacher's handwriting, was the deadname. One form only, we could pass that off as a mistake. But when every permission slip, worksheet, and art project had our child's deadname scrawled in the teacher's handwriting, it was clearly time for another meeting. In the head's office, we came in hot. "What is going on? You told us that we had your support on this, and every sheet of paper that comes home has the wrong name on it!"

Rachel interjected, "You know Kate, it's hard enough to get her to remember to bring home something from school to pass along to us. But when it has her old name on it, it's almost impossible. She avoids that name and wherever she finds it."

The head kept smiling, like this was a simple misunderstanding. "Oh, I'm sure it was a slipup. She's a new teacher—this is her first year! We are so lucky to have her, so we need to be patient."

"Patience comes with consequences. Because every mistake does actual harm to Kate." I was really hoping to preserve this alliance, so I opted to try to strengthen that position. The head was a career educator who seemed to truly care about Kate, and her husband worked across the street from me in the College of Education at the University of Alabama as a faculty member. I hoped I could be logical. "Listen, the research is clear. School is one of the most vulnerable places for transgender children, and it all hinges on how the school supports its students." She seemed to be listening, so I kept going. "I'm happy to collect and show you those pieces of research if that would be helpful. And then, once you've seen the research, we could all talk to the teacher about why these things are so important."

"Hmmm. That sounds good." She was mulling it over. She didn't seem to have made up her mind when she suggested, "Why don't we use the parent-teacher conferences, they are in two weeks I believe, to circle back and talk about this all together?"

Rachel and I agreed, and I got to work. There are only a few times in my life where I've felt that my skills as a debater directly translated into my personal life, but as I began constructing arguments and organizing the research around transgender kids and education, I felt thrilled by how my debate practice was paying off. The end result was over one hundred pages of the most up-to-date mental health and education research. I had bullet-point findings, a summary of specific elements, and the full studies at the end. I organized the research into several connected arguments:

1. Best practice for mental health for children with gender dysphoria and identifying as transgender
2. School as a pivotal space for transgender children
3. Montessori schools as uniquely structured to support these students

I was proud when I submitted it and even received an email from the head that gave me the impression that she had read and agreed with the document. I held out hope that we could do this.

Schooling

A couple of weeks later, we again found ourselves back in those sticky blue plastic chairs sized for first graders and attempted to explain why this mattered. We talked to the teacher about the recommendations of Kate's therapist and pediatrician. We used the analogy of a nickname. We tried to make her understand that Kate very much wanted to please her teacher but misgendering her was causing extreme anguish.

"Listen," she said, "I was a drama major in college, so I've been around a lot of gay people, and I'm just not comfortable using the wrong name."

Not the start we were looking for, for sure. "Who decides the name of a child?" I ask.

"Well, his name is on the PowerSchool forms as—"

I interrupted, "No, who gets to pick the correct name to call the child? Should the child who is being addressed get to pick that?"

"Well, no, not exactly. I think adults should have a say in what children call themselves. Otherwise, I'd have some very strange names in the class."

"So, you think the parents have that authority?"

"I guess, but didn't you pick 'Mac' in the first place?"

"We did indeed. Because we have the sole authority to choose what other people call our child. But picking a name once doesn't mean we can't pick again. That's part of growing up. As a married person, I bet you changed your name as well. Should I call you by your maiden name because I choose to?"

"That's a legal name change. That's totally different."

"How is it different?"

"Because we are required to use legal names."

"No, you're not. Do you use full legal names when calling on a kid in class? How many students go by their middle name instead of their first name? I bet you've got plenty of kids in class who don't go by the names on their birth certificates at all, but some family-friendly derivative. A legal name has bearing in legal matters, not in how you interact with a child in a classroom. A child can be 'Billy' in middle school, 'Bill' in high school, and 'William' in college and beyond. But calling the middle schooler 'William' if they go by Billy would be disruptive, disrespectful, and wrong. Names represent a stage in development. Just like a child who has a cute nickname in kindergarten doesn't mean they have to go by 'Pumpkin' or 'Tater Tot' for the rest of their lives."

"I'm sorry," she stammers, "but I'm just going to have to disagree with you."

"You are welcome to disagree with me." I try to take a breath here. "We do not have to agree. You can think me a terrible parent who is doing everything wrong. But you can't do harm to my child. And based on all the evidence from pediatricians to psychologists to therapists, that's what's happening when you deadname my kid over and over again."

"Well, I just don't see that." She sat back and crossed her arms. She lifted her head and looked to the head of the school, who had been silent this whole time. I knew I wasn't going to get much more time to speak.

"Tell me, what would you call it if I started addressing your son by a different name? If your son decided to take debate class with me, and I decided that he didn't really feel like an Anthony, he felt like a Nancy, and so I called him Nancy every day in class, how would that feel?" Wanting that to sink in, I turned to the administrator and asked, "Would you allow that? Or would you consider that bullying?"

When the head didn't answer, I turned my eyes back to meet the teacher's. Neither will answer—the head, I think, because she wants to support the teacher and keep us in the school. The teacher won't answer, in my mind, because she knows there isn't a good answer. And she's angry now. She's pissed that I would bring her child into it. Good, I think. Maybe this will sink in now. I shift my gaze to the head, who is now squirming and making uncomfortable sounds in an effort to interject without interrupting. "Do you let your teachers bully students?" I ask her. "Of course not. If I called Anthony 'Nancy,' you'd tell me to quit. If I called a child anything that upset them, you'd have to have a problem with it. That's what's happening here. So why can't we pick what you call our child?"

There's no good answer to this question in support of her argument. The reason there's no good answer is that the child and the parents have naming authority, which makes sense from both a liberal and a conservative ideological standpoint. Conservative ideology is built on individual freedoms and the authority of families, not an institution like a school, to make decisions about what's best for them. Thus, it's a conservative position to say that the individual, not the government institution, should decide what's best for them to be named. From the standpoint of a liberal ideology, a greater community of experts have determined that the welfare of the child is clearly at stake, and so the best course of action is to reduce the harm to the child, even if it disregards an individual's, like the teacher's, strongly held beliefs. Again, that would mean that the name should be in line with the recommendations of Kate's pediatrician and mental health counselor. I don't care if your ballot is as blue as a bluetick hound or as red as Bryant-Denny Stadium on a fall Saturday, there's no good rebuttal to this question. The ground this teacher has left herself to defend is weak and unethical. And like so many of us who find ourselves in the same spot, she takes the ground anyway and pitches her last defense.

"Well, it's my strong personal belief, so I must call him 'Mac.'" Her shoulders were taut, her arms holding each other in defense and comfort. She refused to engage the arguments. And it really doesn't matter what those "strong personal" beliefs were. She could believe that there was no harm done, so there was no need to change her behavior, or that there was no such thing as transgender children. Inarguably, she's allowed to have those beliefs, whatever they are, but when she ignores the harm her actions cause based on the misguided conception that her "strong personal belief" supersedes the rights and privileges of individuals to name themselves, the calculus is not reasonable in the least. The right to enact personal beliefs ends at the point in which that action discounts the personal rights of others in the community.

Despite this being a logical conclusion, most all of us, myself included, have issues practicing this simple exercise when living in reality. The problem comes up when we don't want to give up our personal beliefs, and we search for any moral or ethical reason why we should get to keep enacting them, even when it does harm to someone else. There's a significant amount of wonderful research from psychologists that deal with *moral reasoning*. The concept of moral reasoning is pretty simple: We are not logical but emotional creatures, so our internal compass points us to what we are comfortable with, and we justify it as logically as possible.

Sure, we like to think of ourselves as reasonable and logical creatures. I love the idea that my logic and my ability to think through problems is the "why" for all my choices and actions. In situations where we find ourselves dealing with issues that are taboo or that make us uncomfortable, we tend to abandon reason and logic for our ethical or moral compasses. We think we use our logic to steer our actions, but it's often our emotional reactions that steers us in one direction or the other, and our logic attempts to keep up.

There's a wonderful line of experimentation that asks people questions about behavior that would make them uncomfortable that illustrates this conundrum. A researcher might ask a participant about a neighbor that has a dog. It's a sweet old dog, and clearly the neighbor takes good care of it and loves it dearly, but one day the dog dies. The neighbor is distraught and takes the old dog inside, cleans it, and cooks it for dinner. The researcher would then ask, "Is there anything wrong with this behavior?" Almost all the time, the answer from the participants is "Yes, that's not right." Interesting things come from the follow-up questions the researcher asks, like, "Why?" Here, participants struggle to give an answer. They intend to use the logic that helped them make the choice to explain the choice to the researcher, but since they didn't use logic, it's not there. "Well, it's probably illegal," they say. Or, "It's not hygienic." "What if a dog had a disease?" a clever person might come up with. But when pressed and told things like "It's not illegal or unhygienic and it doesn't harm anyone to eat the dead family pet," people tend to hold fast and reply something along the lines of "Well, it's just wrong." They want to have logic to justify the visceral judgment and condemnation of this act, but there isn't a logical reason available, so they are left with only their emotional responses with ethical overtones. Does this sound familiar? I can't speak to your logic, but I have strong feelings that tells me that this is unethical. You see, the other main line of questions that researchers use, other than taboos around eating pets, involves sex. Questions about sex, one of the most taboo parts of our culture, generate this moral-reasoning reaction in participants. "I just know it's wrong, but I just can't explain why" is a common answer in these experiments. When people have a "strong personal belief" about something they think is taboo, they can't engage their logic because it's not what led them to that conclusion.

For Kate's teacher that day, her moral reasoning was blocking her ability to think logically. So no matter how well I debated or how logical my arguments were, I wasn't going to be able to convince her to change her behavior. But knowing what was happening didn't make me feel any better. This was what I was supposed to be good at, and I was trying my best. But I was clearly failing.

At this point in the meeting, the administrator attempted to move the meeting back to our child's progress in the class. The awkwardness was visceral, especially as the head jumped back and forth between using "Mac" and "Kate," unsure of who to piss off.

My guess is this shift into classroom mode was in the plan before we got there, to help the new teacher reestablish authority after the first half of the meeting. It did not work.

As the teacher listed Kate's academic strengths, such as reading and intellectual curiosity, and her social strengths, like being kind to everyone, I could feel myself grit my teeth. The strides Kate had made in the last few months were quickly eroding, both in the classroom and at home. She had stopped doing her homework and dreaded going to school and would cry when she came home from school and told us about her day. When the teacher started in on Kate's areas of improvement, I almost exploded. Pretending like this meeting was about Kate's behavior and success at school felt as if the teacher were shifting any blame for Kate's classroom behavior away from how she was treated.

"I'm having communication problems with Mac," she said in a concerned tone and inflection clearly practiced in the mirror at home, which, after the front half of this conversation, only made it sound more sarcastic than sincere. "Sometimes, he acts like he doesn't hear me or doesn't want to answer me," she said.

"I know the feeling," I thought, "since you are refusing to listen to or answer me in any meaningful way." But I just stared at the teacher. I needed to understand if she was seriously confused or unaware of the linkage here.

She continued. "Mac also has trouble taking work home and bringing work back. We've been missing his home folder for a couple weeks now, so please keep an eye out for it at home."

"It's not at home," my wife said. "It's somewhere here at school."

"So is the problem," I wanted to say, but didn't. My wife had had enough. I could tell by her tone that she was ready to leave.

"Lastly, I think he was having a little bit of trouble with his friend Susan, but I think they worked that out." She said it with a lift of inflection at the end, like the barb on a hook.

Susan was new to the school that year, and since she was the only other little girl Kate's age in the first- through third-grade classroom they shared, Kate desperately wanted to be best friends with her. This child was not a nice child, often picking on the younger kids at the school and breaking up the games of the older kids at recess. Already, in the first few weeks of school we had heard plenty about Susan. A few days before that conference, Kate had come home sadder than usual. When we pressed her, Kate told us that Susan had refused to play with her unless she could call her "Mac." So, instead of having no one to play with, Kate told her it was all right.

There's more to it. Susan had started going to the school that year, so she had been introduced to our child as Kate and had never heard the name "Mac" until the teacher had shifted to using it in the classroom. In fact, the teacher had encouraged her son to use "Mac," and the other kids had caught on. This was why we were seeing the joy and the confidence that had been swelling in Kate in just a few months within the supportive bubble of church, family, and friends reverse course. She went from loving school to feeling sulky and disheartened in a matter of weeks. But what really pissed me off was that an adult refused to see the actual harms her personal choice was doing to a child. So when she wrapped up with "I think he and Susan are good now," I could no longer hold my tongue.

"You know, all those problems you mention come from the same place. Based on what you've told us, it's clear you're not calling our daughter by 'Kate' in the classroom. Is that correct?"

"I don't see what that has to do with Mac's areas of improvement," she said.

"It has everything to do with Kate's areas of improvement. Perhaps she doesn't want to answer to the wrong name in class. Perhaps she doesn't want to bring homework in when you write the wrong name at the top of the page or bring back work with 'Kate' written at the top if you're going to mark it out and put 'Mac.' And perhaps her friend would call her Kate, as she wishes, if that kindness and respect were mirrored by their teacher." With that, we got up to leave and made our way to the door. Holding the classroom door open for my wife, I noticed a purple folder slipped behind the bookshelf closest to the door. I instantly recognized it as the take-home folder, just like the one missing from our household. Even before I plucked it from between the wall and the bookshelf, I knew why it was there. Sure enough, "Mac" was written across the top in black marker. I showed it to the teacher. "I found the folder."

"How did it get there?" She let slip, then covered her mouth in recognition.

"Kate hid it there because you wrote the wrong name on the top." We left before I became too angry to say anymore.

That night, we were informed by the administration that, while they loved our child, they cannot force a teacher to do something against their strongly held personal beliefs. It's a lesson I would have to learn over and over again. Winning the argument with logic is not always the path to changing someone's mind. If I was going to protect my child, I had to get them out of that environment.

We started shopping for schools. We looked at both public and private options. The public schools in our neighborhood looked good and came recommended by many of our neighbors, both educators and administrators, who knew the rules, regulations, and pitfalls a public school faces working with a child like Kate. On one hand, Kate's records would be legally protected from curious parents, we were told. Public schools in the area are required to keep most personal information well protected. But when it came to accommodations, their hands were pretty clearly tied. They were required to adhere to state-verified records. So, if the name change was official, there was no way a teacher or principal could challenge the name by which the child was called. Likewise, birth certificates would determine appropriate restrooms. If you've done the legal legwork to change your child's name and birth certificate during their transition, much of the administrative red tape can be cleared away, becoming a buttressing form of support.

Kate was just beginning her social transition and had not yet achieved these legal milestones, so public school was probably not going to be a supportive space. Private schools have their own drawbacks. Many of the private schools in our area were religion-based, and nearly all were socially conservative in that Christian manifestation. We heard horror stories from other parents of queer and transgender kids, including expelling queer kids who came out.

Schooling

Others were just plain expensive. Sending a child to private school in Birmingham at that time cost roughly the same as sending a child to the University of Alabama. But knowing private school was probably the best place for our kid, we made the sacrifices. We downsized our house and moved to a new part of town where we could send one kid to a private school and one to the public school and started looking at the few remaining affordable secular education choices. On that list were two more Montessori schools for elementary kids. Touring the first one, I asked where the kids use the restroom and was told there were single-use restrooms in every classroom. I thought that was a good time to remark "Good, because we have a young transgender child, so privacy in the bathroom would be welcome."

At the end of the tour, the administrator gave us a single application form. Rachel asked, "Should we put both kids on the same form?"

"No. We will only be considering your youngest child. We would not be a good school for your transgender child."

It's never easy to hear that your child is not welcome in a space, but it's better to hear it before you pay the deposit.

At the next Montessori school, we made sure to mention early in the conversation with the director that we had a transgender child.

"Okay." He seemed unphased. "We have limited experience with transgender children, so I have to ask, what kind of accommodations do you need?"

We talked about single-use bathrooms. We talked about privacy. We talked about support and using her name and pronouns, even if there was another name on her state records. We talked about her safety, particularly from bullying. It felt like we were pounding him with a water hose, not that we meant to overwhelm him, but his reasonable tone and honest questions were a welcome relief from outright rejection and hostility. To his credit, he handled our frantic requests with grace, assuring us that what we were asking for was not much different from what was provided to every student at their school. I had to take a second job to cover the expense of the school, but it was totally worth it.

The school was primarily an elementary school, and Kate ran out the clock at that school, staying all the way through sixth grade. As part of their graduation ceremony, Kate and the other children gave speeches. Kate worked on hers for weeks, partially because she likes performing and partially because her dad knows a little something about public speaking. She crushed the speech at the ceremony, had parents laughing and teachers crying. Sitting in the audience with our family, I kept thinking, "This is what school is supposed to do." There was my daughter, holding the audience captive with crushing punchlines and touching wisdom, because she had been afforded a learning space in which she could be herself and still be celebrated, supported, and encouraged to grow.

At this point, we thought we had a handle on school. We knew what to look for, what to expect, and what to demand. Kate was back to loving school and learning, and we had faith that we could carve out the environment our kids needed in Alabama. And while a significant amount of our optimism came from Kate's elementary school experience, we had reason to believe that her middle and high school experiences could be even better. Heading into seventh grade, we learned that a new charter school was starting up in Birmingham. The school was called the Magic City Acceptance Academy, and it was specifically started as an affirming school environment for students who had faced bullying and discrimination or a lack of resources in their other schools. For kids who were queer, children who were neurologically divergent, and students who were otherwise negatively singled out or left behind, MCAA offered an excellent education that was free of charge and open to anyone in the city.

As we learned about the administration and staff, our optimism grew. Most were career educators looking for a way to improve what they saw as a blind spot in our education system. Others were first-time teachers who felt compelled to sign on to the school's mission of inclusion and diversity, being queer themselves. Better still, we knew people who attended and worked at the school, including our two close friend-families. My friend Daniel was going to be teaching history for the high schoolers, and my friend Allan's oldest son, Carter, was transferring in.

New schools always have issues, but when the students, parents, teachers, and staff are focused on the same issues, solving the issues becomes a whole lot easier. For instance, by this point, Kate had legally changed her name. The school had her listed as Kate in its records, but the state of Alabama's school record system, called PowerSchool, had not bothered to update her name. So when the roll sheets for all the homeroom classes were printed, the sheets listed the deadnames for a bunch of kids, Kate's included. We caught the mistake when Kate's schedule came home, and we called the school. After a couple of conversations with administrators, we helped create a way to the names-check the names of students whose forms didn't match the names listed in PowerSchool. But some students discovered the mistake in their first class on the first day of school, which might have been a total disaster if their teachers and classmates weren't interested in advocating for them. When my friend Daniel got his roll sheet and read off the first wrong name, the student said, "Please don't call me that, it's my deadname." Caught off guard by the administrative mistake, Daniel began with an apology and then shifted to a student-led exercise in introductions. His opening-day lesson plan, along with the printed roll sheet, went straight into the trash, but his pivot exemplified the mission of the school. Feeling empowered, students shared more than their names and pronouns, adding why they were at MCAA, what they had faced in other schools, and what they hoped the year would hold. From there, Daniel shifted the conversation to how individuals, communities, and leaders interact with systems. He not only empowered his students to advocate for their needs but also walked them through how that can happen in a context they understood, their homeroom classroom. So from day one, the students felt they could invest energy in making the school a better place, and their teachers would support them in it. We felt it too.

Because of the mission, the student population, and the success in working with LGBTQ+ students, MCAA quickly became the queer school in town, even as straight students found a home there too. Maybe it was their rainbow staircase, but students of all stripes became comfortable at school again after years of mistreatment. So, while less than 10 percent of the school population identified as transgender and the majority of the students identified as cisgender and straight, MCAA was an excellent school for Kate and many others because of its intentional inclusivity. She loved her teachers and classmates and got to participate in the high school play, *Seussical*. Watching a bunch of LGBTQ+ students and allies shouting "We are here!" like Horton the Elephant's Whoville residents was just a little on the nose for these students in the Alabama public school system, but we ate it up. It was pretty awesome.

The thing about systems, though, is that they are structured like video games. You might be able to fend off the first villains and beat the low-level bosses, but as you progress through the game, the boss battles get bigger and harder to beat. Systems work the same way. If you beat back part of it, chip away enough at the outside, you unleash the wrath of those who benefit from those structures. The boss battles get bigger. For MCAA, tackling the systems that disenfranchise queer kids drew the attention of politicians for all the wrong reasons.

That year was the beginning of an election cycle in Alabama, and the Republican gubernatorial primary featured an incumbent and two legitimate challengers. The Democrats had candidates, too, but the state was so staunchly Republican and gerrymandered that there hadn't been a Democrat in the governor's mansion since Don Siegelman left office in 2003 and they threw his ass in jail afterward. Since 2010, the statehouse has been a supermajority for the GOP. In 2023, the Republicans made up 27 of 35 seats in the senate and held a 77-to-28 seat majority in the house. Of course, it's important to note that the Democrats were the conservative party in the state for much of its history. George Wallace, along with his wife, Lurleen, was a proud Democrat in the statehouse and on the national stage. Systems are about maintaining control, and if a rebranding is needed to do that, so be it.

But in 2021, Governor Kay Ivey found herself running against the usual slew of primary candidates from all walks of life, with her biggest challenge coming from Tim James. James is the son of "Fumbling Fob" James, a star running back at Auburn University and governor of Alabama from 1978 to 1983 and again from 1995 to 1999. Claiming both insider and outsider status afforded Tim James name recognition and critical opinions along with a tendency to hearken back to those good old days, which are all good fodder for raising money and drumming up voters. More concerning was Ivey's political standing. Ivey had taken office following the disgraced departure of her predecessor, Governor Robert Bentley. As a staunch conservative who gained office on his morality and family values platform, Bentley proceeded to have a loud and poorly hidden affair with his political adviser and communications director, which quickly spilled into public view when it became a workplace issue. Rumor has it Bentley's secretary had to move her desk away from the wall she shared with the governor's office in order to not hear what was going on in there. A few misappropriated state-funded trips—including sending the helicopter to get his forgotten wallet when he stormed out of a fight with his wife while denying the affair and some wife-captured audio and text messages between Bentley and his mistress—and Bentley had to step down. True to form in Alabama politics, Bentley made sure to stop and plead out to misdemeanor campaign finance charges related to paying his mistress before coming back to the office to resign. In a state accustomed to political embarrassments, this one was tougher than most.

When then–Lieutenant Governor Ivey took over as governor, she was seen as a political unknown and a soft touch. Her nickname, "Governor MeeMa," perfectly encapsulated the perception of the appointment: As a short, white-haired, bespectacled older woman, she looked like your grandmother. Her public appearances fed the image. She came across as harmless, not totally with it, and just happy to be invited to wherever it was she found herself. So when she ran for election to retain the office in 2021, she carried very little incumbent momentum. Tim James's strategy was to outflank Ivey on the right. Under Governor MeeMa's watch, the state was slipping from its conservative principles and core values, as the stump speeches went. In a political world where mask mandates were a sign of government overreach, these culture war arguments resonated with many conservative voters. What James needed was a concrete example in Alabama, something that linked Ivey to this cultural slippage. But Ivey was a rules-following GOP member since way back and sat on top of a veto-proof supermajority, so James had nothing to stick her with at first. Finally, he found an example of government-funded social depravity: the Magic City Acceptance Academy.

As the first public school in the country to include LGBTQ+-affirming language in its mission statement, MCAA was an outlier in the state's public school system and a sanctuary for so many students. It took MCAA three years of applications to finally be approved as a charter school, and even then, the funding legally afforded was squeezed and siphoned away by politicians and the public school system. But most of this happened out of the public eye, until James's team discovered the existence of the school. In the spring of 2022, James started featuring the school in his television ads, including pictures of students and faculty members pulled from the school's Facebook page. In an ad titled "Genesis," James called MCAA "the transgender school" and lambasted Ivey for funding the "exploitation" of Alabama's children and "teaching children that there are 50 genders." Other fringe candidates latched on to the fervor, echoing James's on-air attacks that the transgender school, with its pride flags and drag show fundraisers, was using taxpayer money to ruin children. With multiple ads from multiple campaigns singling out the school, the students, the faculty, and the community directly felt the attacks. Parents had to threaten legal action to have their children removed from the campaign ads, while the principal wrote "this is why we can't have nice things"–style op-eds, pointing out that the majority of MCAA students are not members of the LGBTQ+ community. Physical education classes had to move inside the lunchroom because assholes kept driving onto campus to yell at the LGBTQ+ students about going to hell and to call the faculty pedophiles. Everyone in the school community was on edge, trying to concentrate on graduation requirements, lesson plans, and multiplication tables while keeping one eye on the exits. As a parent, I was terrified that this attention would make the school a target for a massacre. The school was located across from the police station, and security guards were added to the staff, but the site had no gates or fences, so people were always turning around in the parking lot looking for the building next door or down the street. The exit doors were all glass, with floor-to-ceiling windows all along the ground floor, and students came in and out from the parking lot and outer buildings both during and outside of class. From my perspective, the dangers were real and looming. But somehow, my daughter was thriving.

Even with all the outside turmoil and external threats, such as politicians threatening to shut the school down, the students at MCAA were still happy to be there. The younger kids, like Kate, knew that people were targeting the school from the outside. She had seen the campaign commercials and heard adults yelling in the parking lot about hellfire and damnation, but inside the classroom, she felt accepted and safe. With those ingredients, she could still happily learn, which is the point of school.

In speaking with my friends and their families at the school, I learned that the high school students had gone a step further, recognizing and speaking on the community of MCAA as a mitigating factor in the isolation and fear they felt while away from school. When they were at school, they were comforted because everyone was facing the same issues of stigmatization. At their old schools, they felt isolated in their differences, but at MCAA, their differences were unifying.

Eventually, the adults learned to feed on that energy. For those of us without the similar lived experiences of our children, we adopted their community as our own. We learned that if we sought to be true and good community members, then our advocacy would not have to be individual. Gone were the days of each of us having to sit in individual meetings, asking for the system to change just for us. Feeling the power of the community altered the way I think about advocacy and the way it functions to support the individuals within and beyond that community. Thinking about Kate's schooling, I realized that advocacy is not linear. I was focused, for years, on finding a place for my daughter to be educated, and I thought that meant I had to advocate for her. But focusing that advocacy on her, the individual, meant that progress was slow and stilted and easily reversed. If I had focused not on asking "What can you do for my unique child?" but on "What do you do for all your children?," I think I would have understood better why some schools worked and some didn't. You build communities by empowering individuals with support and understanding. Understanding and support comes from recognizing the overlap of values and beliefs, which then leads to the establishment of common ground. Common ground builds communities, and communities empower individuals who are faced with threats, which begins the cycle anew.

5

Exercising Rights

If you've ever been talked into doing a fun but exhausting physical activity for the first time, you have probably experienced that next-day soreness that feels like death. The actual activity itself matters little: waterskiing, pickleball, or ice-skating will all do the trick. It's that your body is totally unprepared for the specific exertion, coupled with an emotional response to keep doing it until you collapse, soldering an activity you never knew you loved with muscles you never knew existed. And the next day, when those same muscles do nothing but rack your body with pain, you blame the experience on the sport. As you try to convince yourself that crawling to the toilet is less embarrassing than wetting the bed, you swear that you will never do the activity again. But you do. You wait a few years, and then you say, "Yeah, that kickboxing class made me sore, but it sure was fun. I'll sign up for another one," and the cycle repeats.

One day in my late twenties, my wife invited me to her Pilates class. I had never been to Pilates, but my impression was that it was a middle ground between yoga and aerobics, where individuals are led through a series of posture-focused bodyweight exercises. Plus, it was only a forty-five-minute class. I ran twenty-four-hour adventure races at the time; I could do anything for forty-five minutes, I reasoned. At first, it was easy. Hell, half the stuff we did was while lying down. But the number of repetitions was off-putting. I'd lift my leg thirty times and think, "Done with that leg," only to be told to "Hold it" on the last rep or "Now tilt your hip for another thirty." As the class went on, I began sneaking looks at my watch, hoping I misremembered the start time and we were closer to the end than we actually were. But every time I would take my eyes off what I was doing, I was shocked to see how calm and collected everyone around me was. No one was tired; no one was shaky. People didn't even look like they were sweating. Meanwhile, my mat looked like a greasy french fry bag, crumpled and soggy underneath me. Even after the realization that I was in way over my head, I deluded myself that I could hold it together and escape the class with some pride. No one seemed to notice that my active dehydrating was terraforming a small swamp on the floor, and I could skip a rep here and there and no one would be the wiser. Sure, everyone looked as if they were pistons in an engine, and I looked like someone forgot to tighten my screws and the whole thing was going to shake itself apart, but everyone was concentrating on their exercises, not on me.

And that's when I started to squeak. The first time it happened, we were lifting our legs while lying on our sides, and about three-quarters of the way through the reps, I let out a cry. It was shrill and quick, the sound a baby rabbit makes when it's deep enough in the coyote's maw that the teeth are for grinding.

It surprised me so much when it happened that I hoped I had only imagined it. But my wife was looking dead at me with a puzzled look. She had never heard me make a sound like that, and if I had been able to stifle the second one, I probably could have convinced her it was my mat squeaking on the studio floor. But the second pained and whimpering cry sprang from me as stealthy as the first had, already past my lips before my brain could register what my exhausted body was doing. What's worse than the masculinity-crushing whimpers a man makes while trying to lift his leg in Pilates class? The sound of his wife rolling around on her mat laughing freely at him. And yeah, we are still married.

Ironically, I believe a huge strength of our marriage is our shared athletic endeavors. Like many American kids, our lives had revolved around playing everything we could, from volleyball to football, until we began to focus on our favorite, soccer, which we both played recreationally into adulthood. Organized athletics taught us fundamental lessons about ourselves and interacting with others. We learned about physical limitations, perseverance, resiliency, and injury. Sports undergirded our understanding of our own bodies, how they function, and how to celebrate them. Besides pregnancy, which more than half of our population will not experience physically, I can't think of another cultural ritual that champions the function and achievements of bodies more than sports do.

If these early sports lessons taught us how to be better individuals, our later lessons in athletics taught us how to be better partners. We met at the tail end of Rachel's undergraduate years, and many of my athletic experiences after college were with my wife. We played intramural soccer together while she was in grad school, ran and biked together, and did a lot of backpacking and paddling. One day, Rachel saw this flyer for a local adventure race, called the Coosa River Challenge. At that point we had never heard of adventure racing but learned it was a coed team cross-country and off-road triathlon–style event that usually involves mountain biking, orienteering, hiking/running, and paddling, usually over a long distance and for multiple hours, sometimes days. It was a grueling sport involving all our favorite things to do, and because most adventure racing calls for coed teams, we were basically required to do it together. We were immediately hooked. Over several years early in our marriage, we ran twenty to thirty races ranging from eight to thirty-six hours in length all over the country. It was the best marriage training I could have ever asked for. We knew to listen to each other when exhausted, filthy, and lost in the woods during all-night races. We learned how to check on each other, when and how to support each other, and when to give each other space. We developed a team mentality that trickled into the other aspects of our marriage. Getting puked on by a baby after several days of very little sleep feels very similar to the hurt locker of endurance racing.

While I don't suggest using adventure racing as a development tool in every budding relationship, it makes sense that it worked for Rachel and me. Sports and athletics, and particularly how gender overlapped in them, were foundational for my wife and me as we grew up. We both started out on coed teams, and Rachel, because of her athleticism, stayed on them much longer, playing with the boys' squad until she was fifteen and then joining the girls' high school team. She vividly remembers the first male classmate who could beat her in a sprint, Mac Byrd in fifth grade, because up until then, she was the fastest person in her school.

Rachel was athletic enough to earn scholarships at smaller colleges in both volleyball and soccer and walk-on opportunities at Division 1 Atlantic Coast Conference programs. One of the reasons I was originally attracted to Rachel was her athleticism. She was someone I knew I would have to work to keep up with, which became apparent when I tried to join her beach volleyball pickup games. Even though we were dating and head over heels for each other, she would not pick me for her team. I was only allowed to play against her until I developed my setting skills and a decent serve.

This tracks with my life experiences up until this point. Most all my organized sports from middle school on were with cisgender boys, but the women in my family were always ready to challenge the men. My mother's best sport was tennis, and I was required to take lessons every summer so she would not be too bored when she whipped me on the court. She's now older than she'd like me to print, and still, I can count only a handful of victories against her.

These mixed-gender athletic interactions are so important because sports don't just teach us about ourselves. Organized athletics teach us how to interact with others in extremely stressful situations. In sports, we learn competition, sportsmanship, and teamwork. We battle physically and mentally, tracking deficiencies and tendencies in order to prevail, almost always against other people. But we are asked to win in particularly ethical and empathetic ways. Many times, sports force us to communicate, coordinate, and collaborate with others while being exhausted and trying to execute precise movements. Being on a team and working together bonds all different types of people through shared struggle, whether the result is success or failure. Most importantly, we learn how to have fun, even when what we are doing is hard, heartbreaking, or exhausting. Most of us don't earn scholarships, much less salaries, from our athletic prowess, but that doesn't stop us from going out for a round of golf or picking up a softball. Of course, you have to be allowed to participate in the first place to get any benefits at all from sports.

As the father of a transgender kid, I get asked a lot about the participation of transgender athletes in sports, as the banning of transgender athletes has become a common political wedge issue in America. State legislatures across the country have stepped in to ban trans athletes from youth sports. In the name of fairness and safety, thousands of transgender children are officially barred from participation in youth sports like T-ball, mini soccer, and pickleball. As the argument goes, it would be unfair and unsafe to allow someone with male body parts, genes, and hormones to compete against those who have female body parts, genes, and hormones.

I've come to two simple conclusions about these arguments. The first simple conclusion is that most all of the arguments for banning transgender folks from sports aren't new, as they are recycled from similar bans on people of color in athletics. The racial integration of sports in America is a fairly new phenomenon, and there are still pervasive and lingering questions about the treatment of athletes of color compared with their lighter-skinned counterparts. For decades, popular arguments from pseudoscientists claimed that certain bodies were genetically inclined to be disruptive in the spaces of white athletes, posing imagined risks through their supposedly engorged muscles and violent tendencies, allowing segregation to continue longer in sports than in most other cultural spaces. The ghosts of these arguments linger in American sports culture. Researchers have tracked the prevalence of particular adjectives that more often used to describe Black athletes, like "athletic," as opposed to white athletes, who might be labeled "cerebral," and others have noted the remarkable visual parrels between the NFL draft combine and a slave auction. And let's not forget the regular overreactions from the predominantly white cultural power brokers when Black sports stars react to racial discrimination in American culture. Remember Colin Kaepernick, anyone? The National Football League quarterback quietly protested police brutality in America one season and was jobless the next. This is one reason why the arguments for banning transgender athletes from sports seem so tired: We've heard all these arguments before, just while segregating another population.

The second simple conclusion I've made is that adult sports, as a business and culture, is a much more complex and interesting space to have conversations about inclusion, bodies, and athletics. Here, we are dealing with a hierarchical system with competition as its central product. Focusing solely on competition, the hierarchy of a particular sport is a path paved with exclusion. Not everyone makes the roster, earns a scholarship, or qualifies for the Olympics, and everyone seems okay with that. Fans love it, and the athletes at the highest levels seem to understand that their participation is tenuous at best. Even if they are the best in the world one year, they may find themselves cut from the team the next. This makes the issue of transgender athletes in elite and professional sports much more complex and difficult, and thus more important, to analyze. But the vast majority of the state laws passed are specific to banning transgender youth from participating, often with the express goal of protecting the cisgender children. Partially, states target youth sports because that's all the authority they have. In order to justify these bans, politicians lean into images and narratives from adult sports. And yet, when we conflate the business of adult sports, with all its interesting messiness, with youth sports, virtually none of the arguments hold water. That's lazy logic.

But for me, that's where the simple conclusions stop. Because the logic used to exclude transgender children from playing sports is so transphobic, I have a hard time knowing where to begin to succinctly break it down. It's only when I walk through my child's experiences in sports, which began before our state forbade her from participating, that I can explain the consequences of this particular episode of exclusion.

When Kate was young, my wife and I assumed that our love of sports would be a dominant gene, and the pull of organized athletics, and all the wonderful lessons from it, would suck her in like a riptide. The other early signs were there, of course. She had excellent hand-eye coordination and could catch and throw at a very young age. She had fun running with friends, loved to race and chase, and she was a master at tag on the playground. And she had the competitive nature to go with her athletic skill. Kate hated to lose more than she liked to win and would often use every rule loophole to her advantage. I thought for sure we were set for a young lifetime of early Saturday games and late weekday nights of practice. I could not have been more excited, and my wife signed Kate up for her first mini soccer team. This was Kate's first foray into organized sports, and it was an unmitigated disaster.

This particular mini soccer league kicked off in the spring, when Kate was six years old, when the outside world still saw her only as a boy. A few months later, she would begin articulating for us her gender dysphoria and, later, her transgender identity. But that was in the future we could not see, so we had no idea that sports would continue to be a battleground.

Looking back, the dumpster fire of Kate's one and only mini soccer season makes perfect sense. This was not tag on the playground, where all the kids play together and no one keeps score or tracks physical prowess, particularly as it correlates with gender. This was a team of young boys and a coach who used budding masculinity as a motivating mechanism for winning. They were told not to "kick like a girl" and to "toughen up." My daughter retreated, and probably felt trapped or tricked. In her mind, if being good at soccer was indeed masculine, she wanted nothing to do with it. She did not articulate this until much later. What she did, instead, was creatively protest her involvement. When the coach put her in for the very first game, Kate refused to run after the ball. Instead, lest her protest be ignored, she decided on cartwheeling everywhere on the field where she was supposed to go. My wife and I watched, in horror, from our foldout chairs along the sidelines with the other parents we had just met that day. Our older and more athletic child did thirty cartwheels before she was too dizzy to stand, sat for a moment, stood up, and cartwheeled again after the ball. Not two minutes into the game, Rachel looked at me and said, "I'm going to the car."

"Don't you dare leave me here by myself!" I said.

We were mortified and trying our best not to show it, speaking to each other through gritted teeth while yelling encouragement from the sidelines: "Run!" and "Get the ball!" and, finally, "Please kick it!," only to have parents around us laugh hysterically and comment on what fine form she had and that maybe gymnastics was more her sport.

The season continued like this. We talked throughout the week about why trying her best is important for her and her team and what that looks like during a game. But each week, Kate refused to engage the game of soccer as the rules dictate. One week, she pretended to be a different type of animal each time the coach put her on the field. Her first animal choice was a cheetah, which we took as a good sign, until she insisted on trying to chase the ball on all fours. We also saw a gorilla and a lizard attempt to play soccer, neither of which led to team success.

When explaining, pleading, and bribing didn't work, we tried to make her feel bad. We explained that her team needed her and not playing the game the way the team wanted was unfair and mean to the other kids. Not my finest moment as a parent, but if you've read this far, you know it's not my worst either. And it did have some short-lived success. The following game, she stayed on her feet. As a humanoid biped in cleats who did not growl at the other players, she was able to show off her speed and athleticism. Suddenly, the other parents had real compliments, as she blew past players in a sprint. "Okay, here we go!" one parent beside me said with an exhale. Clearly, we were not the only ones growing tired of the constant refusal to be a team player.

For the most part, she did what the coach told her to do. Playing defense, she tracked the progress of the ball and chased it down on turnovers and long balls. Most every time, she was the first one to a loose ball. None of the other offensive players could outpace her, as she had inherited her mother's speed. The only problem was that she apparently decided that kicking the soccer ball was not part of the deal. While she dutifully hounded the ball all over the field, she never once put her foot on the ball. She would chase it down from across the field and wait, only six inches away, as it slowly rolled out of bounds. If it stopped in play, she would stop too and look around and wait for another player to come and get it. As a defender, she would shadow the other player as they dribbled down the field and scored without ever making a move to get between them and the goal lest she come in contact with the ball. The dawning of recognition for the spectators crept across the sideline like a fart. That was our last mini soccer season.

A few months later, Kate began articulating her gender dysphoria and transgender identity. Neither Rachel nor I had played sports with out and open transgender folks, and, at the time, there were no official bans on allowing Kate's participation in youth sports, so we found ourselves trying to figure out how to proceed. We reasoned that Kate would feel most comfortable playing with the girls' teams but knew that competing on a girls' team would probably draw unwanted attention, at the very least. But the idea that organized sports would no longer be an option for Kate was a bitter pill to swallow. Meanwhile, her younger sister was playing every sport she could, following in her mother's footsteps by dominating her male counterparts in flag football. Rachel and I thought, okay, we can find the right fit to make sports work for Kate too. We adjusted our expectations and adapted our tactics. Instead of soccer, we looked for athletic avenues we thought might correlate with our child's situation and still provide the benefits of organized sport. Our next attempt was swim team. She was seven, almost eight, at the time, and had a spent a year socially transitioning into girlhood, choosing what she wore, mostly dresses, in public, growing her hair out, and changing her name to Kate. She seemed like she was in a good place, and we felt like the time was right to try sports again. We chose swimming because we had a neighborhood pool with friends, the parents claimed it was laid back, and most of the kids went to practice but not to the meets. Best thing I can say for her time on the swim team was that she did not drown.

We contacted the swim team based in our neighborhood, talked to the director, and explained our situation. We knew enough to double-check before we got there whether our child would be welcome, and we were assured she would be. The director we talked to over the phone told us they had had "situations like this before," and while we may have to "consider the ramifications" of entering her in the citywide competitions, she would be "welcome at all the practices." After the mini soccer debacle, we were pretty wary of competition anyway, so we quickly agreed that "just practice" had plenty of the potential benefits with few of the potential harms.

But even before the first practice, my wife and I knew that we might be going too far too fast. My daughter was fine with the girl's bathing suit, but the uniform required a swim cap as well. She had been growing out her hair for over a year, and it had become the most important outward expression of her gender. To hide her long blond hair under a cap seemed like a step backward for her. But just like the amateur athlete parents that we were, we tried to make it work and pushed through.

When we got to swim practice that day, I pulled the head coach aside to remind them that my daughter was trans and that I expected her to be treated like the other little girls. I had thought that I was being borderline paranoid, since we had communicated with the director several times in advance of that day. I had assumed incorrectly. It turned out that the director of the program had not spoken with the head coach. The reaction I got was as if I had dropped my shorts and taken a shit in the pool.

"I don't think we have the facilities to accommodate" was the first response I got.

"You mean, you don't have a pool? Because that's all you need for practice, right?" My child was nearby but distracted by friends and excited about swimming on a hot Alabama day. I didn't want this interaction to get heated, so I changed tack. "Look," I said, "I called ahead and cleared it with the director. Kate's not even competing in any meets, she's just swimming at practice."

"Well, I'm still going to have to clear it with all the other parents."

"Clear what?" I was now having trouble keeping my voice low.

"I need to ask the other parents if they are okay with this." He stopped, as if that were sufficient to explain it.

"Are you telling me that parents have veto power over who joins the swim team?" Silence from the coach, so I continued. "Will I get to judge everyone else's kid? Can I base their participation on their genitals? Or are you looking to break HIPAA laws by disclosing the private medical conditions of minors?" My child was in the pool by now, warming up with the other kids. She had no swim cap on; she must've left it in the car. That was in 2017, four years before a transgender swimmer from Penn State University named Lia Thomas would ignite a national debate on the participation of particular bodies in sports. For me, Thomas's pursuit of a national championship in swimming helped clarify why that neighborhood coach did not want Kate in the pool, not because of Thomas's athleticism, but because of her participation. Participation meant inclusion and the disruption of a space reserved for the "normal kids."

Decades before, this sort of intrusion would have led to the pool being drained rather than racially integrate. Yet even as I reflect on the fervent rejection of my daughter simply swimming with cisgender kids, it's important to acknowledge that sports mean a lot to Americans, both as participants and as fans. According to the Bureau of Labor Statistics, Americans on average spend over five hours a day watching, participating in, or reading about sports. Our cultural practices, our communities, even our politics envelope sports culture as a necessary part of daily life. We love the values sports seem to champion, like the American dream ideology that hard work pays off, and it sits well with lessons in patriotism. Whether you are watching a Thursday night junior varsity football game or the World Cup, spectators and players are wrapped in the vigorous and raucous communal support of representing where they are from.

Sports are also engrained as uniquely American in many ways, despite the fact that much of the world enjoys sports like we do. This is partly based on American claims of having invented its three most popular sports: baseball, sometime in the eighteenth century; basketball, in 1891; and football, with its first game played in 1869. Not only do these claims nicely prop up our national patriotism, as we can usually claim international titles in the games we invented and support, but they also stoke the pride of having built something, even a sporting empire, so mightily.

And on that point, the score isn't even close. American sports are big business. In 2023, the industry was worth over $83 billion in North America alone and is projected to reach $260 billion globally by 2033. While industry experts claim several factors in the industry's projected growth, women's professional sports have been isolated by many as a significant factor.

But to make all that sports appealing for consumers, it must center on winning. Americans typically loathe ties and are slow to embrace sports with ties. We construct overly complicated and convoluted overtimes to deal with time running out with the score even. We demand trophies for winners, scoff at participation medals, and keep score from the sidelines for kids' games even when the refs don't. We've built a sporting culture where competition is good and has positive participatory side effects, but only when it produces a winner and a loser. And we feel best about declaring a winner and a loser when we believe the contest was fair. These are the principles that the business of sports in America is built on, and the values and expectations of that product have come to dominate youth sports.

Those who legislate youth sports have borrowed concepts from the professional sports realm to produce a two-pronged argument against including young transgender athletes with cisgender ones. The first argument boils down to this question: How is it fair that a transgender girl competes against cisgender girls? It's built on the scientific conclusion that those with testicles develop more athleticism in puberty than those without and on the problematic assumption that boys are always better at sports. At first glance, this argument makes a lot of sense, because we have scientific studies that seem to back up what we already believe to be true: After puberty, cisgender men have physical attributes that give them an advantage in most sports over cisgender women. But in order for the argument to work, you have to make several illogical leaps. The first is that this argument applies to youth sports as well as to adult sports. But it doesn't. Puberty for most cisgender boys begins between nine and fourteen years of age and lasts until around seventeen years of age. Most cisgender girls start puberty earlier, between eight and thirteen years of age, and puberty ends earlier for girls than it does for boys. This means that elementary and middle school kids are all about the same size and can play together without issue.

In high school, puberty begins to have marked effects. Because puberty begins or continues for most students in high school, it's still not unusual to have cisgender girls who are more athletic and developed than their male counterparts, as well as to have vastly different levels of development among cisgender boys, as some kids grow bigger, faster, and stronger than others. Those vast differences among cisgender boys and cisgender girls are never a cause for alarm or regulation but simply an accepted part of high school athletics. That's because high school sports are still about learning teamwork, self-discipline, body positivity, and other crucial life skills. They kind of have to be, considering that only a little over 7 percent of high school students will find their way onto a varsity college team, and only 2 percent are good enough to earn a sports scholarship to college. So while competition is important for teaching high schoolers life skills, it is not as important to most athletes as the ability to participate is. Arguing that winning and competition are the defining elements of sports at the high school level is again applying an ill-fitting, professional model.

The starkest differences in athletic ability are visible after puberty, when people reach their athletic primes as twenty-year-olds, when they are adults. The vast majority of current state laws that ban the participation of transgender athletes target youth sports. Most youth sports happen before or during puberty, so all that scientific athletic magic juice that makes lasting changes to the body has either just begun to be introduced or isn't present at all, which means it has little to no effect on youth sports. This is why, for decades, coed and mixed-gender sports have been a norm in youth culture. In fact, one could argue that all the way through middle school, cisgender girls are more likely to be taller, stronger, faster, and more coordinated than cisgender boys, partially because they tend to go through puberty sooner than their cisgender male counterparts. Thus, the inclusion of a transgender boy or transgender girl in youth sports would be without significant developmental advantage.

But even when we zoom out to adult sports, we can see that couching the argument in *fairness* misappropriates the concept. First, the word *fairness* is problematic in sport, because while we want the contest to be governed fairly, we don't actually want contestants to be evenly matched. If the games we played were truly fair, they wouldn't produce winners and losers. Rarely would one competitor beat the other if they both had exactly the same skills and approach. What we like about sports is that they are decidedly *unfair*. Sports capture our attention and our imagination because we watch people with various degrees of skill and athletic prowess compete against each other. We watch coaches and competitors develop strategies and plans to take advantage of their strengths and hide their weaknesses. Sports are compelling because we have underdogs,

Cinderella stories, and dynasties that are built only to eventually crumble. Even the greatest athletes must wrestle with the way their bodies break down over time and with the way the game changes around them. Their desperate attempts to stay competitive makes sports entertaining. LeBron James is arguably the greatest basketball player who ever lived, and yet, at the height of his powers, Steph Curry led a quirky Golden State Warriors team to the championship over James in 2015 and arguably changed the game of basketball forever with a mixture of unique skill sets and strategies. But if you were a kid on the playground and you got first pick from a group that included James and Curry, you'd select James for your team. James was bigger, stronger, and much better suited to play basketball in the early 2000s. Was it fair for Curry to have to play against James? Not at all, but it was exactly the fact that Curry was different and used that difference to his advantage that made that NBA finals, and the battles between Curry and James for years to come, so compelling.

Does that mean that fairness should never be considered in sports? Absolutely not. The games should be constructed with fairness in mind. Watching a three-person soccer team take on an eleven-person soccer team might be briefly interesting but ultimately a waste of everyone's time. The sport should be organized to be fair, and it's the competitors who participate that make it decidedly unfair. Thus, the same rules should be applied to and adhered to by everyone participating. That's the type of fairness sports need. Nothing drives a sports fan more nuts than when they perceive the referee to be making calls against one team but not the other in similar instances. But taking the concept of fairness beyond the rules and organization of a sport begins to highlight more abstractions and leads to less actual fairness.

This paradox comes to a head when we attempt to regulate the fairness of athletes' bodies in sports. Randomly unique genes that happen to correspond to our leisure activities can produce world-class athletes. Those physical gifts are not distributed equally among humans. And the more pronounced those physical gifts are, the more the athlete succeeds. Michael Phelps, one of the most decorated and prolific swimmers of all time, barely produces lactic acid when he exercises. Lactic acid is typically the by-product of muscles breaking down during exercise, and it manifests as that burn you feel in your body as you work out. The more acid, the less your muscles work. That's why most people can run only so far for so long. No one else's body in the sport can do what Phelps's body can do (that we know of), so should he be disqualified from competitive swimming because he has a rare and extremely helpful physical advantage? Using a lens of fairness in sports participation is a slippery slope, because each athlete is unique and no two bodies are the same. We seem to understand that attempting to regulate every drop of testosterone, every fast-twitch muscle, and every fine motor skill is not only an impossible task but one that would rob us of the essence of sport. So why, then, have we decided that sex becomes the biological enforcement tool for fairness?

I think the answer is twofold. First, because of the myth that sex is a binary, and second, because of the taboo nature of penises and vaginas. First, the myth of the sex binary, that there is a clear and discernable male body and a clear and discernable female body and nothing else in between, is deeply rooted in our cultures, our social systems, and our laws. Many people ardently believe that humans are born fixed as male or female, and that the designation is both chromosomal and evident through a quick check of our sexual organs. This myth thrives partially because this is most people's lived experience too. They are born with a specific sex organ and identify authentically as the corresponding gender. But the argument of the binary is that there are only these two options, and that's scientifically untrue. Every year, thousands of people in the United States and millions of people worldwide are born somewhere in between, in terms of gender and sex, and we know this because when medical professionals deliver babies, they examine them and keep records, as I've discussed in previous chapters.

An offshoot of this mythical binary is that we assume the difference is stark, comparable, and objectionably measurable. If we feel like we can tell a difference between male athletes and female athletes, we start to develop a belief that we can measure and associate those differences, though we rarely have a full picture. When the sport is based on strength, speed, and endurance, the hormone testosterone is most associated with athletic prowess. Testosterone is produced in varying quantities in nearly all humans throughout their lives, but most humans with testicles experience a significant testosterone boost during puberty, creating lifelong physical changes like facial hair growth, a deepening voice, and muscle development. But does that mean that all people with testicles produce the same amount of testosterone? If not, is it still fair for people with different levels of testosterone to compete against each other? Should we be measuring the amount of testosterone and determining the appropriate amount for fair competition between athletes? And should we do the same for physical advantages unrelated to testosterone, like hand-eye coordination? The point is, isolating a single defining physical trait and declaring it unfair in competition is a false dichotomy, and it hurts both the sport and the individuals who want to participate in the sport.

The second reason why sports are so rigidly divided around sex is the taboo nature of genitalia in American culture. We are, after all, a nation in which Eurocentric, conservative religions took root. Puritans, Quakers, Calvinists, followed closely by Anglicans, Lutherans, Baptists, Presbyterians, and Dutch Reformed, not only sought out the American colonies from Europe for the freedom to practice religion but also worked hard to sustain and promote those values and beliefs as they built communities and pushed farther west. The Congregationalists, separatists of the Church of England, most well known in American history as the Pilgrims of Plymouth Rock, exemplified these ideals of sexual purity along religious lines as well as the move to the American colonies to follow their ideals ardently. The laws regarding sex in their settlement were right out of the Old Testament and included the death penalty for an assortment of lewd behavior, including adultery. Even today, the idea of dividing up the penises from the vaginas comes from the heteronormative and sexual-purity notion that getting sweaty and bumping into one another might lead mixed-sex athletes into sexual "indecency."

Of course, this ignores one of the great benefits of young people in sports: Youth athletics offers an avenue for body positivity, which is getting to know and like our bodies. Currently, body positivity is exceptionally low among children and teens. Up to 46 percent of adolescents in America are dissatisfied with their bodies, and researchers from the University of Minnesota School of Public Health found that body dissatisfaction begins early, before adolescence, and remains a constant concern, at least until age thirty. Body dissatisfaction can lead to all sorts of issues, including depression, anxiety, eating disorders, and even self-harm. But these harms are preventable and treatable, including through participation in sports. Researchers find consistently that participation in youth sports increases self-esteem and confidence, including how kids feel about their bodies. This is particularly important for transgender children like Kate. It was a mighty struggle to get Kate to like her body, and I can understand why.

Watching Kate struggle to understand and love her body, a body that felt counter to what she knew to be true about herself, fueled her mother and me to continue to push sports for her. Soccer and swimming were busts for us, but Rachel and I still felt that Kate needed athletics, particularly as she grew a little older and as her body positivity waned. From another family, we heard about a dojo that their trans son had attended throughout his social transition and how supportive, kind, and thoughtful the sensei had been. Wary after our last debacle, we screened the place thoroughly. Gone were the days of timid probing. Now, multiple stern conversations were standard operating procedure, and after several talks with the head sensei, we were optimistic. Next, we had to convince Kate. Some parts were easy wins. She loved the idea of combat training, as it fit her pretend play so well. She also liked the dress-up part; wearing the required gi, even with the white belt, was a delight. But she had some concerns.

"Who else will be there?" she asked during our pitch.

"I don't know," I said. "We haven't met the class yet, but the sensei is wonderful."

"Do you know if there are other girls in this class?"

"Oh." Shit, I thought. "I mean, karate is for boys and for girls," I stammered.

"I mean, will I be the only girl there tonight?" she pressed.

I couldn't guarantee she wouldn't be, of course, so I had to be careful. "I know from talking to the sensei that there are usually girls and boys in the class, but not everyone comes to every class."

She could tell I was trying to sell her on it, and she became suspicious. "I don't want to do it if I'm the only girl."

She had me. If I made the argument I wanted to make, the "Okay, sure, but being the only girl in the class would be good for you too" argument, there was no way she would go. If I promised there would be girls there, and there weren't, she'd throw another mini soccer animal protest, and I didn't think a sensei, even a kind and supportive one, would put up with that. I knew I could not paint myself into a corner, but I had an ace in the hole. "Well, we can go and see. But remind me to show you the wall of weapons too. When you get to be a blue belt, they train you how to use nunchucks and swords and a staff."

Exercising Rights

Kate's eyes lit up, and I knew we'd at least attend one training. Luckily, at the first go-round, we got a positive surprise. Several of the students were young girls and one of the two younger black belts leading the session was a young woman. We thought we were in the clear. But despite loving it, Kate protested going nearly every time. She'd have to be prodded to get ready, dragged to the car, and nearly pushed through the door. But then she'd get into the dojo and smile from ear to ear while she trained. She beamed when she was paired up with the other little girls. She enthusiastically engaged in the games and the skills and happily progressed through the belts. But no matter how much fun she had at the dojo, she'd beg to quit the next day. We could not figure it out. We started watching practice like we were scouting a rival, looking for flaws and weaknesses or tells that would highlight why Kate never wanted to go back. It wasn't until years later that it dawned on me how stressful it must have been for her to perform feminine in that environment. While no one openly challenged or questioned Kate's girl-ness in that space, there was always the possibility, no matter how slim, that someone might. Sure, karate was clearly for boys and for girls. But was it also for transgender girls?

When she was older, we talked about her karate days, and I confirmed my suspicion. Balancing being feminine enough for her gender and athletic enough to participate with and among cisgender boys and girls weighed on her. Her body made her an outlier, even if she was the only one who knew.

It was around this same time, the late 2010s and early 2020s, when major athletic organizations needed to rethink their rules regarding bodies in sports in the name of fairness. For instance, when the London Olympics were held in 2012, the International Olympic Committee (IOC), which governs international sports rules, broke from the traditional determinations of gender qualification and instituted hormone testing. Up until that point, whether an athlete at the Olympics was in the male category or female category was based solely on their body parts. In fact, it was Olympic procedure in the years before World War II to have athletes parade nude in front of judges before competition to secure their place in their events. But the IOC was being pushed by the recognition of transgender, intersex, and nonbinary athletes, whose identities and bodies did not neatly fit into the two categories. And while the old ways, like the naked parade, were mostly insulated and beyond the eyes of the public, several athletes, such as Keelin Godsey, an American transgender hammer thrower, and Chris Mosier, a transgender duathlon athlete on Team USA, were drawing international attention. In some areas, elite athletic organizations made progress, and a consensus around procedures and a clarification of rules grew more public and robust. But so did the backlash.

Much of that backlash centers on the misuse of the concept of fairness, as I have discussed. But a second, more nefarious argument being made to exclude transgender athletes from sports is safety. The question is framed as "Is it safe for little girls to play with girls who used to be boys?" Or, even more manipulatively, "Would you let your little girl play against a man?" You've heard me spend chapters on how parents protect their children, and so I get how seductive this fear tactic is, but let's break down the logic of this argument. First, it's built on the same assumption as above, that at the youth level the cisgender boys are already developed into testosterone-jacked, strapping men, while the cisgender girls have matured into delicate flowers. While I've talked about that earlier, specifically that we are talking about the legislation of mostly prepubescent youth, not adult, sports, the safety argument takes the debunked assumptions a step further by implying that cisgender boys are tougher than cisgender girls. This is the basis of the legal claim against the NCAA and San Jose State University's volleyball team and protests against the participation of boxers Imane Khelif of Algeria and Lin Yu-ting of Taiwan in the Olympics. In both cases, the unverified accusations of the participation of transgender athletes ran counter to the testing and qualification polices of the governing bodies, but participants claimed that the volleyball player and the boxers hit too hard for women to tolerate. In both cases, the claims were both statistically untrue and overtly patriarchal. The volleyballer in question spiked the ball at about the average pace of the other women in the conference, and far below the speed of college women at elite programs. But these arguments have staying power if we believe that the other women in these competitions need protecting.

That's where the dangerous part of this argument comes into play. If the goal of such legislation is to protect innocent, delicate little cisgirls, it casts transgender children as the aggressors, the harm-bringers. The echoes of this transphobic narrative go far beyond sports and connect squarely to the resources and spaces that cisgender and transgender children share, like locker rooms, bathrooms, and even the schools themselves. In bathrooms and locker rooms, transgender students are far more likely to be the victims of violence than to be the perpetuators of violence. But the idea that transgender students are violent interlopers in education spaces extends to coverage of the most heartbreaking American phenomenon: school shootings. On December 16, 2024, a tragic shooting took place at a school in Madison, Wisconsin. Within less than an hour of the story breaking and before any details about the incident were released to the public, multiple online provocateurs baselessly asserted that the shooter was transgender. As Alex Jones of Infowars notoriously declared to his 3.4 million followers on X (formerly Twitter), "If the statistical trend continues with this tragic event, there is a 98% chance the shooting is trans or gang related." In reality, transgender youth make up 0.11 percent of suspected mass shooters, according to the nonprofit organization Gun Violence Archive, but that miniscule statistic fails to correlate with the outsized accusations. Jones was not the only media mouthpiece to openly suspect that a transgender youth had targeted cisgender classmates, nor was this the first time the tactic was used following a school shooting, with NBC News capturing the trend after shootings in Houston in February 2024, in Philadelphia in 2023, and in Uvalde, Texas, in 2022, none of which included a transgender-identifying perpetrator. Capitalizing on a trend that baselessly links transgender youth to violent crimes, these viral public accusations reverberate across more than just fringe media sites. After Jones's comments involving the Madison shooting, former U.S. Representative Matt Gaetz, R-FL, added to the unfounded speculation when he asked on X why "trans control" wasn't being considered as a response to the shooting, rather than "gun control."

At the time of writing, twenty-five states ban transgender youth from participating in the sport that matches their gender identity, which the Movement Advancement Project reports affects 37 percent of the transgender youth population in America. Not only are these laws exclusionary and run afoul of local and national sports associations but they also put all young athletes, including cisgender athletes, in harm's way. After Utah passed a law in 2021 banning transgender athletes from participation in youth sports, parents began investigating the sex of athletes who beat their own children in races. *The Salt Lake Tribune* in July 2022 uncovered that a school district was secretly investigating the sex and gender identity of a high school track star at the badgering of a rival runner's parents. Apparently, the aggrieved parents argued that the student must be transgender because they were too fast, as they kept beating their child. But a story like this is not an isolated event. In upstate New York, a parent watching a flag football game assumed that an athlete was trans (they were not) and livestreamed their rant accusing the young person of cheating and identifying them, opening them to public ridicule and the threat of violence. In British Columbia, an elderly spectator reportedly yelled at an event volunteer to prove that a nine-year-old track-and-field participant with a pixie haircut was really a girl after berating the fourth-grader herself.

In addition to these witch hunts, the harms of exclusion from the community of sports should be enough to turn a parent's stomach. The majority of parents, 88 percent, believe that sports benefit their child's physical health, and 73 percent believe that sports improve their child's mental health. Parents of kids who play sports know that it can have lifelong benefits that go beyond health, with 55 percent believing that sports help their kids succeed in school and careers. But most importantly, parents of athletes recognize what it means for community—80 percent of parents believe that their children learned to get along with others through sports. That's corroborated by independent studies, which showed marked increases for young athletes in empathy, negotiation, empowerment, self-control, leadership, critical thinking, and resilience. If youth sports have health benefits and build stronger communities, why should anyone be excluded?

In 2018, after dramatic exits from soccer, swimming, and karate, my daughters finally discovered roller derby. Roller derby is a female-dominated physical form of roller-skating in which competitors wreck each other while coordinating blocks, passes, and scores in a circular rink. Competitors wear pads, and helmets are required, because injuries and gruesome accidents are common and are typically cheered on by the beer-soaked spectators. The local Birmingham team, the Tragic City Rollers, built a queer-friendly kids' squad called the Tragic City Troublemakers. Both of my daughters, then ten and eleven, embraced the Troublemakers with zeal and reckless abandon. In roller derby, players take on call signs, probably to divorce themselves from the violent personas often required for roller derby bouts. Evelyn became Princess Lei-Her-Out. Kate was known as Luna Shovegood. Thank god for roller derby. Not only did both my daughters get to practice, push, and press against their personal limits of physical ability and those of the kids around them but they also saw kids of all sizes, shapes, gender identities, and genetic makeups try to win games of physical skill, effort, and strategy.

For the first time, I watched with hopeful optimism as my trans daughter let herself embrace a sport. I saw it coming together at practice. She skated hard, enjoyed being sore, got knocked down, and jumped back up. She was comfortable being athletic and a trans girl with her team. But having sat here before, I still worried that she would hold back when match day arrived. The upcoming match with the Chattanooga squad would be open to the public, and I wasn't sure her comfort and joy would be enough for her to push through. And Kate's success in practice brought the opportunity for scrutiny. Through her hard work, Kate earned a chance to be her team's jammer. The jammer is pitted against the other team's jammer as one of the most important roles on the squad as they race each other around the track. If one team's jammer laps the other jammer, a point is scored. Everyone else attempts to set blocks for advancing their jammer and for disrupting the other team's jammer. It is the most closely watched and scrutinized position on the squad, so much so that the jammer's helmet is marked with a star so everyone, from the competitors to the audience to the referees, pays extra attention to them. And suddenly, my transgender daughter earned the role. Deep down, I assumed that at any minute, she'd put on the brakes for fear of being outed and ousted. I had seen it play out, I believed, even for elite athlete on the biggest stages.

Caster Semenya is a world-class sprinter from South Africa. In 2010, at nineteen, she was taking the track-and-field world by storm. After winning the world championships in Berlin, she went into her gold medal press conference unaware of the rumors spreading, mostly from anonymous competitors, that she was just a little too masculine to be running with the women. In that press conference, a reporter asked Semenya if she was aware that officials were conducting a genetic test to judge her femininity. Clearly blindsided, she asked the reporter to explain. Apparently, under the guise of a postrace steroid test, race officials had conducted a controversial genetics test, unbeknownst to her.

Semenya was a presumptive favorite at the London Olympics in two years, but suddenly, she was deemed too masculine to race. What followed was a nebulous and secretive testosterone therapy requirement from the IOC, the first of its kind as far as the public knew, and a very public feminization public relations campaign for Semenya, including a magazine spread with the headline "Look at Castor Now!" to display her new feminine makeover. In the article, Semenya fielded questions about motherhood, cooking, and even hair care. Gone were the pictures of the Olympic-hopeful sprinter flexing her muscles in victory, with six-pack abs and broad shoulders, and inserted were the soft hair and flowing dresses of the traditional housewife in waiting. I cannot fathom what Semenya weathered in order to be deemed feminine enough to compete in the London Olympics. I know it involved heavy scrutiny of her testosterone levels, despite having all the physical parts to normally be deemed female by Olympic oversight. It probably didn't help her that she was Black and African, while many of her public accusers were white and European. Then the Olympics came, and despite being chosen as the flag bearer for South Africa, the pressure on Semenya to balance gender norms and athleticism started to show. Hardest to watch was the 200-meter finals, her specialty. Semenya had qualified comfortably, but in the finals the pressure seemed to smother her. Watching that race live, and several times on repeat, I saw a sprinter breeze past her competitors, and then, checking that she was solidly in second place, pull up. She cruised to the silver medal. As sad as it made me, I can't say that it surprised me. It is exactly what I expected my daughter to do. Self-preservation over achievement.

When the day of the roller derby came, we brought a robust crowd. Get a Baptist preacher from the South in a sporting crowd and watch out. Along with our associate pastor, we had an Ethiopian preteen, an adopted teen, and an assortment of queer and straight footballers, soccer players, and basketballers who knew our daughter when we thought she was a boy and when she wore a girl's bathing suit for the first time. And they were screaming their lungs out when she skated her ass off. She blew by blocks, got knocked on her ass, and mixed it up like a kid full of the energy that uniquely comes with team sports. When a jammer scores and can strategically halt play, they double tap their hips with their hands, palms to the sky. It looks and feels like a celebration. Seeing

Luna Shovegood skate through the line and pump her hands in celebration stands as one of those singular moments we all hope for as parents, when you can watch your child strive and succeed. And Kate's success was not about winning. It was about being in a sport that celebrated and embraced the athlete she was. The trigger for her success after so many failures was that she did not feel like the only out-and-proud queer person on the team and that everyone was celebrated for being exactly who they were together. Why would you deny that to any child?

By now, you have heard about the walks Kate and I take, and those have replaced organized sports. We will drop my youngest off at practice—she's a competitive climber now—and Kate and I will walk along the river. She doesn't participate in roller derby anymore, and that's okay. She knows she can if she wants to, because Luna Shovegood taught us all more than I ever dreamed she could. Kate knows now that she can be her authentic self, which includes being transgender and athletic and goofy and resilient and a valued member of a team. What more could a parent ask for?

6

Seeking Health

The first time Kate got puberty blockers, she passed right out. We were on our second or third visit to the gender clinic at the Children's Hospital in Birmingham, and it was finally time. The way it worked with our insurance was that the medicine was delivered to us, but because neither my wife nor I had experience injecting medication, we made an appointment with the endocrinologist and enlisted some professional help. They were amazing, talking Kate through the process in caring tones, prepping her for the shot, and distracting her expertly. She was absolutely thrilled to get the puberty blockers, and we were walking the hallways toward the exit when she reached up and touch my elbow and said, "I don't feel so good."

"Are you messing with me?" I asked. Even as I asked it, I could tell she wasn't. She was turning into a wet noodle right in front of me.

"Noooooo . . . ," she said as she collapsed. Somehow, she managed to sound like someone falling even as she fell. Luckily, because I was right there and on the alert, I caught her as she went down and scooped her in my arms before she hit the floor. The nurses and doctors were all over her, and she came to quickly. The doctors concluded that while the syncope episode, also known as *passing out*, was medical in nature, it had nothing to do with the medication. After some careful probing, it became clear that Kate had skipped breakfast in hopes of stopping on the way to the gender clinic for fast food. We had said no to her request, but it didn't dawn on us that her gamble on a breakfast stop would trigger a medical scare. Now it was almost noon, and the excitement for the treatment and the prick of the needle, combined with her low blood sugar, were enough to kick her nervous system into overdrive. "We all handle stress differently," Dr. Ladinsky told us. "She's been anticipating this moment for years, and that stress, even happy stress, has a physical effect on the body." Luckily for Kate, the gender clinic was housed within the children's diabetes center, so they were well stocked with blood-sugar-balancing supplies. A bag of Cool Ranch Doritos and a cold Dr Pepper later and she was as good as new, except for a budding fear of needles.

 This was probably Rachel's and my first real glimpse at how and why health care matters so much for our family, not just in terms of the specific care needed for our child but also for the physical effects that stress has on your body. As I've talked about previously, the first few years of Kate's life as Kate meant little to no change in medical care. Kate had a mental health therapist and a supportive pediatrician, and she needed nothing else. Social transition certainly rubbed up against social and cultural expectations of gender, but the physical changes involved, like growing out her hair, were simple and noninvasive. But Rachel and I knew, sooner or later, we'd have to deal with puberty, and the conversations about medically altering her body to align with her gender would come with much more significance.

The first thing I want parents to know about this part of Kate's journey is how complex this issue feels. We struggled mightily with what medical intervention looked like for Kate. For one thing, every transgender and gender-diverse person is on a unique transition journey, so medical care can look drastically different from one person to another. One person may need puberty blockers, a completely reversible treatment that buys time to assess their mental and physical needs. An adult may opt for a type of gender-affirming surgery, which can be as simple as reducing the prominence of an Adam's apple or as complex as a vaginoplasty. Electrolysis of facial hair, mastectomies and breast augmentation, vocal cord shortening, and gender hormones like testosterone and estrogen are all options for folks who want to take steps to align their bodies with their identities. But while many options exist, they are not all required for or chosen by everyone or even available to many. People are forced to make choices about what they need to be themselves authentically based on health care availability and cost and the pros and cons of each medical intervention. And while there are several out and visible transgender celebrities, media coverage of their gender journeys often focus on the result, not the process. Remember when Caitlyn Jenner debuted on the cover of *Vanity Fair* in June 2015? Jenner had disappeared from the public eye while undergoing gender-affirming surgery, only to reappear *transitioned*. For noncelebrities, gender journeys are probably more stilted and may last years, decades, or even lifetimes. For

Kate, and I assume for many other folks, each transition decision is complex, where each step is weighed and assessed over restless days and sleepless nights.

In our case, we needed as much time as possible to address the options and consequences of certain interventions. Puberty blockers are exactly what they sound like: They halt puberty as long as they are being taken, and puberty restarts when they are discontinued. But our next anticipated step, using hormones to overpower male puberty and induce elements of feminine puberty, came with life-changing impacts, including sterilization. We told ourselves we wanted Kate as mature as possible before a decision like that was made. In reality, we were scared to death of doing something she might regret. Most medical interventions at this age feel high stakes. Parents agonize over things like their children's piercings. How many piercings are too many for a teen? What will people think? Can they still get a summer job, a scholarship, or a spouse? These are reasonable concerns, and I wish I shared them. Instead, I'm left to ponder if my daughter will regret, years from now, not being able to contribute sperm to an embryo or carry a child, because the best care available to treat her gender dysphoria comes with the side effect of sterilization.

I'm not blind to the ramifications of gender-affirming health care for children, but I believe what every major health organization has concluded, that gender-affirming health care is the best thing for children experiencing gender dysphoria. At the very heart of our parenting choices, Rachel and I are attempting to treat Kate's gender dysphoria. Medical experts will tell you that gender dysphoria manifests as an intense feeling that your body, or parts of your body, contrast drastically with who you are. According to the American Psychiatric Association's *Diagnostic and Statistical Manual of Mental Disorders*, gender dysphoria is defined as a patient's "marked incongruence between their experienced or expressed gender and the one they were assigned at birth." An article published by the National Institute of Health notes that gender dysphoria is associated with higher rates of self-harm, interpersonal conflict, decreased self-esteem, and higher rates of suicidality. The medical community seems to have come a long way toward understanding and treating gender dysphoria, though listing it in a manual of mental disorders gives me pause because calling it a mental disorder reeks of stigmatization. Still, gender-affirming medical care stems from understanding the social and physical impacts of gender dysphoria and working to reduce or eliminate those negative outcomes.

For Kate, gender dysphoria fit everything we were seeing and experiencing behaviorally, and it had felt like the dangerous behaviors that result from untreated gender dysphoria were right around the corner. We saw the self-harm begin, and it scared the hell out of us. And as soon as we began treating Kate for gender dysphoria, she became a happy, healthy kid again. But the thing about gender dysphoria is that it may never fully go away. Kate was happy now, sure, but treating her gender dysphoria as a ten-year-old was going to look different from treating her gender dysphoria as a fifteen-year-old, thirty-year-old, or sixty-year-old. Consider this: How much effort does it take to manage the body dysphoria of cisgender teenage girls (and boys)? With the ridiculous beauty standards pushed by Hollywood, the fashion world, and social media and our American ideals of fitness and health, our culture sets nearly unattainable goals of what young people should look like. Working to meet those standards creates an immense amount of pressure on young people. Add to that having a body that doesn't match your authentic self, and the tensions are exponentially increased. This is what happened in our household. We knew, logically, that shifts in treatment were going to have to coincide with how she felt and the care available to her as she got older.

For the most part, Kate's gender dysphoria manifested in two distinct ways. The first was with her hair. When Kate first began her social transition, her hair was the most important part of her identity. She grew it out as long and as fast as possible. If I had told her that eating slugs would make it grow faster, she would've wolfed down dozens of those slimy suckers. Her hair signified for her that she rightfully belonged in the world of her gender. This was indisputable in her young mind. On our very first trip to the gender clinic, we met the doctors for the first time, and Kate said as much. Kate was probably eleven years old at the time, far from puberty, but Rachel and I wanted to understand and be ready for the next stage. As we sat in the examination room with the doctors and nurses, the endocrinologist, Dr. Ladinsky, explained to Kate, "It will probably be a while before you see me again. I will help with your hormonal transition."

"But I've already transitioned," Kate said. For her, growing her hair out and telling friends and family that she was a girl was it, the end of her transition story.

"Of course," Dr. Ladinsky said. "Kate, do you know what puberty is?"

"Yes." She answered with confidence, but did not elaborate.

"Well then, you know that puberty causes your body to change. Those changes come from hormones that are inside your body and make your body look different, your voice sounds different, and you even smell different!" She crinkled her nose at this, and Kate giggled. She continued, "Because you still have some boy parts, your body is going to go through boy puberty. That results in a deeper voice and facial hair. Look at your dad." She gestured to me. "Do you want a beard like your dad?"

"No!" Kate was practically shouting. Talk about inducing nightmares. Turning into her father was her worst-case scenario. Sheesh.

"Exactly." Dr. Ladinsky continued. "So, we help pause boy puberty and start girl puberty. Does that sound better to you?"

"Yes, that sounds a lot better." Kate was exuberant again. At first, I thought she was exaggerating for the audience, but as Dr. Ladinsky turned the conversation back to the adults in the room, I watched Kate follow the conversation with a fixed attention that was rare for her. Leaning forward with eyes narrowed in concentration, she was engaged. She wasn't hamming it up. Kate was trying to retain every word she heard, transfixed with the conversation and, simultaneously, squirreling away information to unpack later.

Kate's rapt attention is like a drug for me, as I am often frustrated by her glossed eyes and wandering mind. She often claims she doesn't know something that she was told ten minutes before. I joke with her that she is that old *Far Side* cartoon that shows a dog owner talking to their puppy, but all the dog hears is its name. So while the owner is explaining to the dog not to chew his shoes, the dog only hears "Fifi! BLAHBLAHBLAH. Fifi, BLAHBLAH-BLAH." Most frustratingly, Kate always acts like it's the first time she's heard about the cartoon, even though I've told her this several times. Either she doesn't remember because she wasn't paying attention or she knows it tortures me to pretend like she didn't hear me the first time.

At the clinic, I was hypnotized by her concentration. It was only when Dr. Ladinsky began talking about measuring testicles that my own attention snapped back to the conversation.

"Orchidometer beads." Dr. Ladinsky was explaining. She went over to a drawer in the examination room and pulled out what looked like a lopsided pearl necklace. The white beads start as small as a pea, followed by incrementally larger beads, the largest of which is the size of a quail egg. "This is how you measure the testes to know when puberty has started," she said, and dangled the beads in front of me to see and then in front of Rachel, who had probably asked a relevant question, and then dropped them in Rachel's lap. I'm not sure if she wanted to handle them, but she cupped her hands at the last moment to catch them. I almost laughed out loud, but I got a look at Kate's face next, and my laugh died in my throat. She had clearly understood the purpose of those beads and was already horrified at the prospect of having her private parts regularly inspected.

We've always treaded lightly around Kate's "boy parts," as she called them. Specifically, Rachel and I talk about anatomy in age-appropriate ways, including how to wash or where to check for ticks. But Kate's body had become an emotional minefield, another physical trigger for her gender dysphoria. She often made it clear that she didn't want to talk about her body parts, which is a pretty easy subject for all parents to mostly avoid. But as we approached puberty, she began to avoid being naked as much as possible. Mostly, that meant that she avoided bathing. We'd encourage, we'd threaten, and we'd bribe, but getting her to shower was a regular battle. Even caring for her beautiful long hair was not enough to tip the scales in favor of voluntary showers. Then here came puberty, and she had started to smell. Everyone does, sure, but Kate was smelly and refused to shower. It got bad enough that we worried she might lose friends over her musk.

Because that's another piece of puberty, right? Kids get weird about their friends. New cliques form as some kids get interested in romance, others stay in sports a little longer, and some seem to become popular and then are excluded overnight. And how would friends feel about a transgender kid now that they were becoming more and more interested in sex? In the preteen years, sexual attraction was not a major factor, but puberty ushered in the idea of boyfriends and girlfriends, which made the issue of disclosure vastly more important. Could this be another opportunity for rejection, maybe even violence, for Kate? We had no idea how this might shake out for her, but we were worried that puberty might reduce the ready support she had come to enjoy from her friend group.

Kate's social transition prepared us somewhat for her physical one, but not so much that we were suddenly comfortable with what it might entail. To cope, I also stepped up my engagement of transgender health care from a professional angle. Part of what I research at the University of Alabama is the communication that takes place within, among, and around folks facing health care stigmatization and disparity. Early in my faculty career, I was lucky enough to be included in a multiuniversity interdisciplinary research team called Trans Collaborations focusing on the barriers to health care for transgender adults in rural communities. Based at the University of Nebraska, with hubs at major research universities in the Midwest and the Deep South, the program sought to establish community partnerships with transgender, gender-diverse, and gender-fluid folks to reduce the barriers to health care in places where options were already limited. Several noteworthy projects came from this collaborative work, but working with a diverse group of transgender and gender-fluid adults and hearing about their experiences trying to access care without being stigmatized was a cornerstone of all our research projects. One of the projects we were asked by our community partners to create and implement was a workshop to build confidence, self-efficacy, and resiliency for health care–seeking transgender adults. One of the most important things I heard firsthand from our participants was that each and every one had encountered health care situations that made them feel scared, ashamed, or stigmatized. In the best instances, they encountered professional and courteous health care workers who did not know how being trans would affect their particular aliment, so the patient often had to play educator. Even when the doctors had a grasp of how being trans may or may not affect treatment, they often lacked the nuanced bedside manner needed to provide truly gender-affirming care. In one community project, we ran simulations of appointments for our transgender participants, and we would hire medical students to come in and play doctor. Many of the medical students stopped me after the project and begged for additional training, articulating that so much of their education was diagnosis and treatment and almost none was intercultural communication. But in these projects, even while volunteering, they could connect the link between a positive communication interaction and the likelihood that a patient would get better.

But well-meaning doctors and nurses were not the stories that haunted me as a researcher and a parent. I also heard horror stories of transgender women being forced to take pregnancy tests, of a broken foot becoming a recommendation for psychological intervention, and many, many attempts to arrange conservative religious counseling instead of prescribing things as simple as flu medication. In the worst situations, our participants revealed that they left vowing never to return, often shunning care even in dire medical situations.

Most of the research I've read confirms the accounts from our participants: uncomfortable, intrusive, and combative health care happens much more often to queer folks, and these incidents lead to the reason why queer folks seem to rely heavily on their networks to navigate health care systems: it functions to protect and to advocate for the patient. Having done a significant amount of research in transgender and gender-diverse communities, I heard over and over again that seeking health care almost always required community support to ward off negative encounters. For instance, a mental health center may claim to be "trans-friendly" on its website, but community members routinely told me that they would not even consider going unless they knew someone else who had tried the center. Considering the amount of available and well-hidden conversion therapy out there, I was not terribly surprised. What did surprise me was the way systems have adapted to these cultural norms. For instance, when we first began trying to track down the gender clinic at Children's Hospital at the University of Alabama in Birmingham, not one of the operators we talked to knew what we were asking for or which department to transfer us to. Luckily, I had sat on a panel hosted by a community advocacy group about gender-affirming health care with a children's endocrinologist, who gave me a direct line to one particular nurse. "Call her," I was told, "and say your daughter needs a Tuesday appointment with Dr. Ladinsky." And then we were in.

This is how we got to the gender clinic at Children's Hospital in Birmingham. The gender clinic was a gem but a hidden one. Something I've learned from talking to trans folks about their experiences in the medical system and through our own journey is that queer people rely heavily on intracultural networking when it comes to health care. There are two reasons for this. The first is practical: best care. Queer folks make up a health-disparity group. Empirical studies show they are routinely underserved or poorly served in our health care system. Having or anticipating negative experiences in health care affects us and makes us not want to go back. Best care does the opposite, in that we trust our health care team and we are more likely to follow instructions, advocate for ourselves, and have better health-related outcomes from care (that is, get better). Best care almost always means affirming care. If you go to a doctor who scoffs at your "lifestyle" or questions your authenticity, it won't be a good experience, even if they are a great doctor.

The second reason for these health care networks is emotional: It's a way of showing love. Queer folks, especially transgender individuals, are frequently thrown out of the house, disowned, or abandoned by family members. The Trevor Project, a nonprofit research and advocacy group aimed at reducing suicide among queer kids, finds that 28 percent of LGBTQ+ kids find themselves homeless or facing housing instability. That number jumps to almost 40 percent for trans kids. Facing down a serious medical condition is difficult for anyone, but without the support of family, the struggle becomes even more daunting. But I have witnessed outpourings of support, including visits, appointment rides, home care, and all the other tangible signs of love and support, from people connected through their queer community. Luckily for our family, that love and support often embraced us as well. For example, when my father was in the hospital recovering from heart surgery, one nurse friend, Christa, whose wife and daughters had become like our family, inserted herself in my father's recovery room and was at his bedside at every free moment, despite the fact that she worked in a totally different part of the hospital. The surgery was not a total success, and she relayed information to us in the waiting room, interpreted charts and results, and acted as an advocate for him when we could not be in there with him. In her scrubs and mask, she blended into the scene of the hospital room, and oftentimes, visitors had no idea she was anything more than a nurse on the floor. In reality, she was his comfort and his shield when he needed one badly. Even through the times when my family could not be with him, she used her connections, knowledge, and authority to love him as a proxy for us. He died a few days later, and it gives me so much comfort knowing that he had Christa there with him in those excruciating days.

I'm convinced that these tactics of care within the queer community, of which I have limited but profound personal experience, come from decades of operating in systems designed mostly for cisgender straight people. As the family of a transgender child, I can say that we unabashedly leaned into the privilege that our social status and identities allowed us in order to find care. In fact, I'd say that we sought care fervently and at all costs, for fear that it might disappear. As it did for my family and the hundreds of other families with transgender kids in Alabama beginning in the fall of 2021.

In 2022, the state legislature proposed a bill making it a felony to seek or give gender-affirming health care to children. Senate bill 184 was quickly passed and signed by the governor and hailed by conservatives in the state as a win against liberals in the culture war.

I don't love using the term *war* in situations like this because it seems to justify dehumanization and violence toward someone you disagree with. I have never experienced war myself, and it seems to me that those who use it flippantly haven't either. But the actions of the legislators in Alabama forced our family into a state of fight or flight. We lived like we might at any moment have to pile into the car and drive to a safer state or get into a fistfight over the bathroom our kid uses at the grocery store. The thing about fight or flight is that it's supposed to be temporary—either you escape and your body settles back into its normal rhythms, or you die and it doesn't matter. But living in a state of fight or flight stresses your body constantly, like extra pressure in a pipe. Eventually, something is going to bust. For me, it was my heart.

In the summer of 2021, my heart gave out during a round of golf. Luckily, my foursome included a friend who was a doctor and willing to do chest compressions for about five minutes after I collapsed. At that point, he got my heartbeat started back, and I began breathing again.

My doctors will always associate, at least chronologically, the stress associated with my sudden cardiac arrest with fear of COVID-19, as it was the largest health crisis of most people's lifetime and was still ravaging populations around the world in the summer of 2021. But there was another important health crisis at that time that probably links with my heart failure more than just chronologically, and that was Kate hitting puberty just as the state of Alabama took away her access to health care. So when my cardiologist would ask "Are you experiencing a significant amount of stress?," the answer was unequivocally "Yes, yes I am."

The goal of health care is and should always be centered in the Hippocratic oath, which includes "do no harm." If only legislators were held to a Hippocratic oath.

7
The Dragon

A good buddy of mine named Richard can smell bullshit a mile away and will not abide it. We met in the PhD program for communication at the University of Alabama. While I would often note, or simply wince, when a classmate said something off, inaccurate, or illogical, he would speak up and ask them to explain their way out of the misstep. He would even do it to our professors, which endeared him to some and made him a villain to others.

Richard and I remain close friends, despite his regular moves around the country as he is promoted, headhunted, and redistributed through the levels of higher education leadership. Our two most common conversations, when we aren't collaborating on research or catching up on each other's families, involve where he is currently interviewing for his next promotion and why I'm not also on the job market. Because, while he continues to add titles to his office door and zip codes to his forwarding addresses, I have been pleasantly immovable at the University of Alabama, starting as an undergraduate, then a master's student, then returning for a PhD seven years later, and finally becoming a faculty member, a post I have held (as of this writing) for eleven years. Add in the years I spent as a student, and I have been a member of the same department for twenty years. I like to joke that the only person who has been in our department longer than I have is our indispensable department secretary, and neither of us has tenure!

"There's a tenure-track job posted, did you see it?" Richard would say. "It looks like they read your CV and then wrote the job call to match. It would be a huge step up. You should just apply and see what happens. You can always just use it as leverage if you got it and didn't want to go."

All of these were perfectly valid points, and for years I'd attempt to beat them back with logic. It played directly into Richard's hand.

"Bullshit!" he'd declare.

And he was right. After a few years, he made the same arguments so often that I didn't even bother to refute them. "I don't want to move. I like it here. My family likes it here," I told him.

"There are lots of places y'all would like," he'd say.

"This is my home."

Richard could only smell the bullshit. "Sim, your home state is terrible for transgender folks. And you have a trans kid."

"We have everything we need here and the opportunity to make our space better. What more is there?"

"So what would it take to get you to look for a job and actually move?"

"Richard, I'd have to be on the run from the law." I said it as a joke, and yet it got to the heart of it much more accurately than I would ever know.

When we first caught wind in 2020 that the Alabama legislature was introducing HB 1 / SB 10, which they called the Alabama Vulnerable Child Compassion and Protection Act, it seemed unreal. Targeting health care workers and the families of transgender children, the bill made gender-affirming care, or health care that recognized trans identity as legitimate and not something to cure, a felony to conduct. The legislation was framed as a way to save children from genital surgeries and unproven medical interventions, both concepts that are misleading and fearmongering in regards to the treatment of transgender kids. The bill claimed that certain treatment methods for gender dysphoria hadn't been rigorously studied, despite overwhelming data from every credible health organization in the United States. The bill claimed that gender-affirming care "constitutes dangerous and uncontrolled human medical experimentation that may result in grave and irreversible consequences to their physical and mental health." It apparently didn't matter to the lawmakers backing the bill that surgery for transgender children is not part of transgender care in the state, or that medical professionals and parents were doing what experts say is best for their children's long-term health. Over multiple iterations of the bill, lawmakers continued to try to define the issue in their own terms. This was our home, our lives, and our family. Everything and everyone we loved was here in this state, and now the state was attempting to take away our child's access to health care. We had no choice; we had to fight.

 I first heard about HB 1 / SB 10 from our child's endocrinologist. We were working on a research project together that involved training young doctors about gender expression, and she told me that the bill was being shopped around and that Alabama was looking to try it. At this point, in the fall and early winter of 2020, no other state had yet passed legislation targeting transgender children. This was before bans on youth sports participation, before Texas decided that parents who affirmed transgender kids should be investigated for abuse, and before we were even out of the COVID-19 pandemic, though those legislative maneuvers soon followed. Conservatives in our state started the school year furious about mask mandates in schools and vaccines against COVID-19, firmly convinced that parents should have total control over the medical choices for themselves and their families. It seemed bonkers to me that the same people who claimed that their right to get COVID-19 should not be infringed on by the government could turn around immediately to claim that the government should dictate the health care path of a child.

Our endocrinologist passed our contact information on to a lawyer from the National Center for Lesbian Rights (NCLR), which does LGBTQ+ advocacy around the United States, and we got a call in January 2021 about the bill. The lawyer's name is Asaf Orr, and he was the director of the Transgender Youth Project at the NCLR. He walked us through HB 1, which targeted anyone and everyone who provided gender-affirming care to transgender youth, including doctors, parents, pharmacists, and even schoolteachers and counselors who might advise a student struggling with gender dysphoria. Providing the best health care for transgender children, the state seemed to believe, should be a Class C felony. Like robbery with force, stalking, and looting, this Class C

The Dragon

felony designation came with a minimum sentencing of one year and a day and a maximum of ten years in prison.

In our first conversation with Asaf, he framed the call as twofold: letting us know what national advocacy groups like his were seeing and getting to know us to see if we would be good plaintiffs to sue the state to stop the bill, should it pass down the road. Asaf told us that Alabama and Arkansas were both considering the legislation at this point, but all signs pointed to Alabama being the first to attempt to pass it. So he was looking for a family that could speak to the harms of the bill from that perspective, and we were eager to have the support and expertise of the NCLR as we faced down this dragon.

More than anything, Asaf was using the call to get to know us. He asked us about ourselves and our lives. What did we do for work and fun, had we always lived in Alabama, and what were our social circles. He asked a lot about our family, and especially Kate, how we felt about having a transgender child, when did we know she was trans, and how did she tell us. Asaf was doing his best to understand as quickly as possible who we were and if we'd be good clients. I genuinely believe he was calling to help us, but it felt like an interview too. But Rachel and I felt like a fight was coming, and we wanted Asaf and the NCLR as allies.

In some ways, Rachel and I felt like we had been preparing for this fight for quite some time. We had navigated school, family, church, and hundreds of daily moments of advocacy for the past five and a half years, as Kate was now twelve years old. But all the battles we had fought up to this point were mostly private. They were strategic choices for small-scale victories in tight, insulated communities. We often told Kate that being transgender did not have to be a secret, but it was still private. We had been careful with that private information. Now, we had to make what was private more public. And as ominous as this felt for Rachel and me, Kate clearly could not comprehend the ramifications. At this point, everyone she knew and loved already understood and respected her identity. She had no concept of the larger, darker world that lay just outside our well-guarded familial borders.

And so much was on the line now: home, church, school, careers, and friends, and we were about to put all our chips in the middle of the table and call. Hell, I work for the University of Alabama on a renewable contract. What are they going to think if I sued the state? Even now, I'm convinced that writing this book about being a dad puts my job on the chopping block.

We held out hope that it would not come to that. We viewed working with the NCLR as precautionary. It was a way of preparing a lawsuit for only a worst-case scenario.

As we feared, both the house and the senate of the Alabama State legislature presented bills to criminalize seeking and administering gender-affirming health care in February 2021. It was clear to me from the beginning that the sponsors had no genuine sense of the life experiences or needs of a transgender child or the best practices of health care professionals. When SB 10 was introduced on the floor on Groundhog Day of 2021, the sponsor, state senator Shay Shelnutt (R), of Trussville, almost immediately showed his ignorance on the subject.

The Dragon

"What is gender dysphoria?" Shelnutt said. "I looked it up. According to the Mayo Clinic, it's a feeling of discomfort or distress that might occur in people who have a gender identity different from their sex at birth." With a quick internet search, you can find something very close to this as the first line on the Mayo Clinic's website in an article titled "Overview of Gender Dysphoria." To Senator Shelnutt's credit, this is not a bad definition to start with, though it's not quite an exact quote. But that's where the senator's research stopped, at the very first line. Because if Shelnutt had read past the very first sentence on the Mayo Clinic's web page, he would have found that the rest of the information, including the section on treatment and diagnosis, ran totally counter to the arguments he wanted to make. Maybe he did read further than I'm giving him credit for, because he changed tack. If the Mayo Clinic isn't going to say what you want it to say, then you'll have to make something up. And that's exactly what the senator did. "My definition," he proclaimed, "is someone thinks they should be a girl if they're a boy or thinks they should be a boy if they're a girl."

Why did Shelnutt need his own definition? Here is the crux of the legislation: If all the research says that gender-affirming procedures are the best treatment for gender dysphoria, then the institutions cannot be trusted. The insistence to ignore the definitions, research, and conclusions of one of the most trusted medical institutions in the world and instead make up a definition for something that Shelnutt claimed no expertise or experience in highlights the tactics behind these laws. From the very beginning, framers of the bill attempted to contradict, challenge, and misconstrue the information from the most trusted medical groups in America in order to vilify transgender people and their supporters.

Using his own definition instead of the Mayo Clinic's was only the first alteration of established medical findings. Shelnutt continued to assert on the floor of the senate that "science shows that children that are going through this gender dysphoria, most of them mature or grow out of this stage if they are given the chance"—a totally unfounded claim that ignores the consistent findings of decades of ethical research on the subject. By definition, gender dysphoria is not a phase but a serious long-term mental struggle. But claiming that "science" was on his side, he could then fight the way he wanted. "So why is [this bill] needed?" he continued. "It's just to stop these surgeries and these drugs on our children." Again, no gender-affirming surgeries on transgender children are performed in Alabama, but that inconvenient truth might reduce the fear needed to fuel his conclusion. "[This bill is] to protect our children. That's my simple explanation." Simple is too kind a word. "Disingenuous" comes to mind. So do "willfully ignorant" and "bald-faced lie." But the intent behind that first speech on the floored laid bare the political intentions: Stigmatize the care, ignore the science, and scare the people.

I still held out hope. If the issue boiled down to how best to protect children, the bill would fail. My aim became to emphasize that point: The transgender children of Alabama are only in danger when they lose access to health care.

After HB 1 (which became HB 303) and SB 10 were introduced in 2021, they were sent to committee for consideration. HB 303 went to the Judiciary Committee, and SB 10 landed in the Health Committee. The Health Committee held a hearing open to the public, and word spread among the stakeholders that we'd get the chance to speak on the bill in that meeting. I drove to Montgomery with the intention of speaking. A close friend, who was studying community health and communication, drove to the capital with me. I recently asked her what she remembers about that day, expecting some details about the proceedings that I had missed. Instead, she said, "I remember how sad you were. I remember you practicing the speech you were hoping you'd get to give, and how we both cried in the car. I thought getting there was the hard part, but it was even more sad afterward."

We arrived thirty minutes early, and the meeting room was packed. Many who were not early were turned away, and most chose to sit in the hallways or walk the sidewalks around the building in solidarity with those inside. Most importantly, the crowd was overwhelmingly against the bill, as was apparent by counting the transgender and rainbow flag–style pins and buttons that adorned the otherwise professional dress of nearly all the attendees. Once the doors were closed, the legislators set out a sheet of paper for those who opposed the bill and those who supported the bill to sign up for an opportunity to speak, for up to three minutes each, about the bill. There was a bit of a scramble because so many people wanted to speak, and it quickly became apparent to me that people had positioned themselves close to the podium for this very reason. Once I got to the sheet of paper from my seat in the back, only three people had signed up to speak in favor of the bill and more than thirty had signed up to speak against it, with many more behind me in line. When the paper was passed to the chair, he said, "Well, it's a pretty even split in favor and against, so we'll limit the speakers to the first three for and first three against." It was such a bald-faced lie, even his colleague called him out on it later in the meeting by having those in attendance raise their hands either in support of or in opposition to the bill. But it set the tone: We who want the passage will only believe that which helps the passage of the bill.

The first speaker was one of the sponsors of the bill, though I do not remember which. What stuck with me, however, was his insistence that children were being mutilated. The bill, he insisted, was to prevent more Alabama children from having harmful surgeries. After his remarks, one of the committee members asked, "How many surgeries of this kind were performed in Alabama every year?"

"I'm not sure, I'll have to look that up," he replied.

When an endocrinologist from the gender clinic at the University of Alabama at Birmingham–Children's of Alabama Hospital was asked the same question at the end of her remarks against the bill, she gave the true answer. "None," she clarified. "There are no gender dysphoria–based surgeries on children or youth performed in Alabama. It's a dangerous myth used to scare people unfamiliar with gender dysphoria. Those surgeries simply don't happen ever in Alabama."

After the bill's sponsor, it was a doctor's turn to speak in favor of the bill; I believe he was either a psychologist or psychiatrist, if my memory serves. He claimed that a study from Johns Hopkins University showed irrefutably that gender reassignment surgery was not necessary and could be harmful. This so-called study has been used for decades as anti-LGBTQ+ ammunition. Among the paper's claims were assertions like being gay is a choice and transgender people don't actually exist because gender identity is an "elusive concept." The paper, authored by two professors at Johns Hopkins University, Dr. Paul McHugh and Dr. Lawrence Meyer, isn't itself a scientific study but an awkward attempt to reinterpret the findings of other scholars to fit their beliefs about the LGBTQ+ community. Published in 2016, not in a medical journal but in *The New Atlantis*, a conservative think tank's periodical, and without peer review, which would have involved outside experts who vet the claims and methodology in scholarly research, the paper misconstrues legitimate research to bolster the beliefs of the authors, neither of whom had conducted independent research on LGBTQ+ Americans. The problems with the paper are profound and widespread, and scholars have spent years debunking its claims and conclusions. Even though the paper was wholly discredited within the medical community, it continues to be presented as scientific evidence in political situations targeting the rights of LGBTQ+ folks.

While the doctor speaking in favor of the passage of the bill sounded good, he also had trouble in Q and A. It turned out, he didn't actually work with children, youth, or transgender folks in a professional manner. He worked with adults and stated that he himself had never worked with a transgender adult who had had gender-affirming care as a child. Nor was he even from Alabama; I think he said he was based in Canada. The more he talked, the more it was clear to me that this doctor was brought in for his testimony, something he's probably done many times.

The next speaker in favor of the bill similarly felt out of place, as she was not from Alabama, did not receive care in Alabama, was an adult when she received care, and did not have surgery. Nonetheless, her message was deemed crucial in making the medical case against gender-affirming care. This person shared a story of detransitioning. She had felt that she was transgender, received gender-affirming treatment, and then changed her mind. As a result, she claimed she has had to live with the side effects of the treatment. She talked about doing research online and coming to the conclusion that she was transgender without seeking medical advice. From there, she sought and requested hormone therapy from her primary care physician. She described lingering abdominal pain from the hormone injections and the flippant manner in which they were prescribed by her doctor. She said she still wrestles with the regret.

Detransitioners have become a focal point in these legal and political battles. Despite multiple longitudinal medical studies, including a fifty-year-long study of gender-affirming surgery in Sweden that found that less than 3 percent of people who undertook steps to transition regretted their decision, a single anecdote can be a powerful persuasive tool. Hell, it can be argued that I'm using the same tool, an individual's story, to try to be persuasive. Moreover, I've talked about my own hang-ups about Kate's own transitioning in multiple chapters, even though I fervently believe it is right for her. But when someone else tells a story of misdiagnosis, poor medical care, and regret that can follow, it reinforces the "they'll grow out of it" assumptions of people who are skeptical of transgender folks and throws doubt on the medical community that these bills target.

I believe that the stories of everyone who wrestles with gender identity are important. Where I have trouble with the argument at the heart of this speaker's testimony is the call to action. The arguments from both sides—the people who argue that transitioning didn't work for them and those who argue for lifesaving gender-affirming care—lead to the same solution: access to reliable medical care. Instead, this person explained how they skipped the prescribed best practices of trans-affirming care, and used that as the basis of her call to action against gender-affirming care. I'm saddened that she didn't have this access because it probably would have saved her heartache and pain. Good medical care means following evidence-based best practices. That's important because each case is unique, and patients are complex individuals. The best medical care comes from teams of professionals who find the right balance between relying on research and remaining attuned to the patient. Crucially, gender-affirming care also does not conclude that every person with questions about their gender identity is transgender. And more access to care and fewer attacks on that care leads to better health outcomes for all patients, whether transitioning is right for them or not.

In contrast to the speakers in favor of the bill, everyone

advocating against the legislation that day was directly involved in the care of transgender youth in Alabama or was a transgender youth in the state. A principal in the school system talked about protecting students from bullying. A pediatric endocrinologist from the Children's Hospital refuted the testimony of those who had earlier argued against the bill, claiming that their care was in line with the best practices of every major medical association in the country. A high school student told the committee that without the gender-affirming care they had received, they would not be alive today. I did not get to share our story that day in the state senate, but I was inspired by the people who did.

Yet despite what I felt were compelling stories and arguments against the bill, the committee voted to pass it along to the next legislative step, reconciling it with the sister bill in the house. As the bill progressed, our conversations with Asaf became more specific. He asked us to join the lawsuit he was preparing, and we said yes, anticipating the passage of HB 303 / SB 10. We stayed in close contact with Kate's doctors, working up the courage to ask how we could continue Kate's care if the bill passed, and then taking the question back to Asaf. "Could we leave the state for care?" and "What about telemedicine?" were just a couple of the ideas we tried, but Asaf had the same answer for most.

"I'm sorry, but the bill is vague when it comes to what constitutes the enforcement mechanism but very clear about the consequence." He meant that the bill very loosely defined what gender-affirming care might look like, but if the activity was deemed to be gender affirming, it would be charged as a felony.

"The bill mentions hormones and blockers explicitly, so you are putting yourself in danger especially with those, but we think it's a pretty sweeping ban."

In the end, it was probably its sweeping nature that killed the bill the first time. HB 303 died in the Judiciary Committee, but SB 10 rolled through the Health Committee. All it needed was to be reconciled with HB 303, pass a roll call vote, and get signed by Governor Kay Ivey, but there were only a few legislative sessions left. Time was running out before the state representatives and senators left town, and SB 10 looked less and less likely to pass.

The final session in April came and went without the bill getting a vote. We heard a lot of explanations for its failure. Some said the united front of teachers, parents, doctors, and pharmacists was too much political capital to overcome. Some said that conservatives were simply looking for a culture wars win for that particular news cycle, not a protracted court battle. Still others claimed that the governor had quietly threatened a veto. Others gave credit to our legislators on both sides of the aisle who understood the lasting damage the bill would do to families and to the reputation of the state. Regardless of the reason, we celebrated. And even now, knowing what was to come, I'm glad we did. It's important to know that victories can still happen, even in the face of dragons. But what I didn't realize at the time was the ephemeral nature of the win. Conservatives were simply testing the waters on these issues, not abandoning them. That legislative session in Alabama would became an early blueprint for a deluge of anti-trans legislation that was just on the horizon.

8

Beyond Alabama

The bill to ban gender-affirming care for children was reintroduced in February 2022. We did what we could. I marched around the capitol with advocates, family, and friends while the bill was being discussed. I called my district's lawmakers and contacted the lobbyists I knew. We made sure that everyone who might care about us, about the issue, or about the state knew what was happening and encouraged them to speak out against it. No one offered much optimism. The bill passed with only four votes against, and the governor signed it into law before the end of the week.

I have never felt so abandoned in my life. I am a man of privilege, I know that. I am used to systems working in my favor and people listening and considering what I have to say. Moreover, I am both a student of reason and a believer in the persuasive power of emotional connection. Rejecting this law was the logical, as well as the moral, thing to do. There is no plausible, evidence-based reason to reduce the best possible health care for a vulnerable population, but only four people voted against it. The lives of hundreds of families were broken, cleaving off a necessary resource for the mental and physical well-being of children. Doctors and other caregivers, including parents, were made felons for helping in the best possible way. And no one in the government seemed to care. Signing that bill into law told me that the political bump from a "culture wars" win was more important to my state than my child's well-being. And it hurt all that much more because I love my state. I have defended Alabama against other people's perceptions for decades. I have told anyone and everyone who questioned my home that there were good people here who loved each other and made community in wonderful, diverse, and boisterous ways. We sang in church, hugged strangers in football stadiums, and showed up to support friends and neighbors. These were people who had learned hard, important lessons from discrimination in the past, were working to dismantle the systems of discrimination that remained, and were committed to not repeat those historical mistakes. The people of Alabama, I believed, had seen the worst that humans could be to each other and wanted to be better. But the most hateful legislation I have ever witnessed passed through the halls of representative power as easily as memories vanish from a well-worn mind. No one seemed to remember or reference our past as they concocted asinine reasons to stigmatize vulnerable children, their families, and their caregivers. The good people of Alabama, it seems, were not in the room where those decisions were made that day. Those elected officials seemed to have no memory left to recall the ghosts of our past, no voice to name them, and no guts to stand and vanquish them. This, the failure of the good people of Alabama, is what broke my heart.

• • •

Beyond Alabama

What I didn't understand about living in crisis was the living part. The sun still rises, the days go on, and all those little routines that made breathing feel like living are still there, waiting to be taken care of. My grief and rage over the legislation was like too much salt in a stew; all the normal ingredients were still there and none of them tasted right.

Worse still, we felt more isolated than ever and were recognizing just how much we needed our communities right as they were about to be stripped from us. Our family and friends checked on us, worried over us, and listened. They were wonderful, but they could not wrap their heads around what we were going through. Crisis isolates you, and you see everyone else, even the most empathic, going about their lives, fussing over gas prices or basketball practice or rain on vacation, and I'm stuck wondering if I should be doing the same thing. I felt trapped and in danger, but everyone else seemed okay. That's its own kind of misery.

Our little family unit tucked in tight. We found ourselves being around each other a lot those days and weeks following the passage of the bill. The kids were twelve and thirteen, their screen time was limited, and without any cars, there wasn't any way to get them out of the house. So, with them underfoot Rachel and I did that delicate parental dance of pretending that shit wasn't hitting the fan. We acted like nothing was wrong to keep them from freaking out. Still, there was only so much we could do. The kids were scared, and so were we, but we tried to make things as normal as possible. We ate meals at our kitchen table, played cards and board games, and tried not to talk about it. Most of the time, we felt we were on eggshells and the kids knew it. They stayed on their best behavior, they did not rock the boat. In the evenings, we'd have family meetings in the hot tub. We had made the purchase the year before with the last of the money my father left me when he died. He had had one, and I always enjoyed it, but Rachel took some convincing. "Those things are nasty," she told me. "You won't catch me in there."

She was absolutely wrong. The hot tub almost immediately became a retreat. It was not a big space, it barely fit the four of us, which was just right those days. No phones were allowed, and everyone relaxed in the hot water. We'd sit facing each other and talk, laugh, and be silly. It was the family time we were craving. Everyone let their guard down. In the summer we'd turn down the temperature so we could stay in there longer, soaking deep into the evening. In that cheap, sometimes not-so-hot hot tub, the kids must have sensed that Rachel and I could take a breath, and they started to probe.

"What happens next?" Kate asked one night. We were all in the hot tub, and it was after dinner. It was not dark enough to have the lights on, but she had turned them on anyway, and the water was an iridescent blue. Instead of making eye contact, everyone's eyes were on the water as it swirled and bubbled. "What happens now that the law has passed?" Kate asked again, without looking up.

"I don't know for sure." I did, actually. It's fight or flight. We stay and we do battle or we leave everything behind and flee. But both answers felt too aggressive for the hot tub, or I just didn't want to say them to her out loud.

"Will we have to leave?" Kate said, and she looked first at Rachel and then at me.

Evelyn chimed in, "I don't want to leave."

"None of us want to leave," I said, "but we may have to." They got really quiet then, just the sound of the jets and bubbles as the evening faded around us.

We weren't done fighting, because we still had the courts and the next step was the lawsuit. Asaf and the National Center for Lesbian Rights made sure we were prepared, and, as soon as the law passed, they had filed the paperwork to sue the state with our family as plaintiffs. The NCLR weren't the only ones filing, as other rights groups in the state like the ACLU and the Southern Poverty Law Center also had families, doctors, and counselors opposing the legislation. This was uplifting. It meant we weren't alone, that others were willing to fight a little more, and we began pooling our knowledge and resources.

In addition, I decided it was time to talk to the press. Up until this point, I had spoken with reporters from several news outlets, both local and national, but always off the record or with our names withheld. I knew it was not what the reporters wanted, and not really what I wanted either, but I had to advocate without outing my thirteen-year-old daughter. But it felt like we were losing, and the harms from the passage of the law outweighed the harms of potentially outing her. So when I got a call from the journalist John Archibald from AL.com in May, I answered. I had read his column for years and respected his reporting. I was even more impressed when I read his book, *Shaking the Gates of Hell*, in which he chronicles his family's history of church leadership during the Civil Rights Movement, wrestling with the fragility of good white Christians in a time of racism and hard-fought justice. When I talked to reporters from other places, they always seemed to stop listening at some point and be like *okay, but, like, we all know Alabama is terrible, so why don't you just get out?* In Archibald I hoped to have found a reporter who understood my love of our home and know its issues too. We talked several times about the situation, about my family and the law as it wound its way through the legal process. In the end, Archibald wrote a beautiful piece about my family and this battle for Alabama. The part I think he captures so well is when he talks about why a bill like this, despite the illogic and the obvious harm to children, could pass. He says:

> Perhaps that is the goal of laws like this, to force the different to flee, so that Alabama is devoid of dissent. Perhaps the goal is to make life so tough for those who don't fit a politically popular mold that they find it necessary to find a friendlier place to live. I hope not. The thought of that breaks my heart.

About this time I got a call from a reporter from *The Washington Post*. I had taken several calls like this as national attention began focusing in on the spreading anti-trans legislation, and most were sandwiched in this period of late spring 2023.

I spoke with a Molly Hennessy-Fiske, and we talked about what living in Alabama was like for our family and about the ways other states were similarly passing laws and directives aimed at transgender families. I was at a work event at the time, a public speaking workshop I was leading for new MBA students, and I had to step out to take the call. I had become pretty adept at this dance: professional face off, personal face on, and then professional face back on. I once got a call from the U.S. Department of Justice while I was trout fishing in Arkansas. I took the call in the middle of the White River because it had the best reception, floating in a small boat with the guide. Life happening on top of life.

Hennessy-Fiske wanted to talk about more than just Alabama; she wanted to talk about other states with their own bills. "I've talked to families that are trying to get out. Are you considering the same?"

"Of course we are." I was outside in the heat of midday, which is scorching in the Deep South, even in spring. I'm trying to stay in the shade of the building, trying not to sweat through my shirt, but talking through these things with a stranger agitates me enough that I want to pace. "But how far is far enough?"

It had taken two consecutive legislative sessions to pass the ban on gender-affirming health care for children in Alabama. In those two sessions, from the time the bill was first introduced in 2021 to the time it passed in 2022, America seemed to become a dangerously different place for transgender youth. When Alabama first considered making doctors and parents felons for supporting transgender children, there were few laws on the books codifying the stigmatization and policing of transgender bodies. Now, please don't hear me say that transgender, nonbinary, and queer folks had it easy prior to 2021. Transgender adults still faced discrimination around legal documents, like passports and driver's licenses, significant social and cultural stigmatization, disproportional amounts of violence, and health disparities and had very few legal protections in employment, housing, health care, and other necessary parts of life. But many of these issues were social and cultural. Few laws were on the books to restrict the rights of trans people, and the new ones that were introduced, even in deep red states, found little traction. For instance, before 2021 no state had legal bans on trans children participating in youth sports, requirements for school counselors and teachers to out students to their families, or any of the other anti-trans legislation we've seen from 2021 onward.

But the legislative session of 2021 functioned as a national inflection point, where the number of bills targeting transgender youth almost doubled across the nation, from 85 bills to 155. In addition to Alabama, one other state, Arkansas, had serious momentum that year behind a bill to limit gender-affirming health care for youth. While the Alabama version died in committee, the Arkansas bill passed, though it faced a veto from then-governor Asa Hutchinson, a Republican, who called the bill a "vast government overreach." Arkansas eventually overrode Hutchinson's veto and passed the first state legislation banning gender-affirming health care for youth in America in the spring of 2022. With that passage, the dam seemed to burst. One legislative session later, bills that targeted transgender youth in health care, sports, schools, and bathrooms were introduced in state legislatures across the nation. In 2023, state legislators considered 615 new bills targeting transgender youth, an increase of 253 percent over the year before. This trend continued in 2024, with 637 new anti-trans laws considered by legislators.

That's not to say that there were no laws restricting the rights of transgender people before 2021. We only have to go back to 2016 to see a trial run when North Carolina passed the first bill restricting public bathroom use to the sex listed on a person's birth certificate. But the passage of North Carolina's house bill 2 (NC HB 2) ended up being a debacle for the state. Several high-profile businesses canceled contracts with the state and moved their corporate offices elsewhere. PayPal halted an expansion that would have brought in four hundred new jobs to North Carolina. The NCAA relocated its March Madness tournament games. Performers from Bruce Springsteen to Cirque du Soleil canceled performances there. In total, North Carolina lost an estimated $3.76 billion in revenue from the passage of NC HB2.

The loss wasn't just financial; it was cultural. In the early to mid-2010s, American culture seemed to be shifting away from transphobia. Several television shows prominently featured transgender actors and transgender characters without much of the stigmatization and demeaning depictions that had typically been a feature of media depictions of transgender individuals prior. These included reality shows like *I Am Jazz* in 2015, *Dancing with the Stars* in 2011, and *I Am Cait* in 2015, as well as a host of Emmy Award–winning fictional shows like *Pose* in 2018, *Orange Is the New Black* in 2013, and *Transparent* in 2014. NC HB 2 ran into a rising swell of popular media, including a stunningly successful grassroots protest dubbed #WeNeedToPee. These viral social media hashtags were made up almost entirely of transgender people taking selfies of their experiences following restroom laws like NC HB 2. In some of these, you could see masculine-presenting protestors sharing the space with befuddled and uncomfortable cis women. In others, feminine-presenting protestors took pictures with urinals in the background. In each, the message was simple and clear: The law put me here. The argument was visceral: In an attempt to make people more comfortable in bathrooms, the law was doing the opposite by forcing trans people to out themselves in restrooms.

Politicians in North Carolina felt the backlash from HB 2. The Republican-controlled government faced a very vocal condemnation that led to the downfall of the previously popular governor, Pat McCrory, who promptly lost the next election to a Democrat, Roy Cooper, despite Donald Trump carrying the state in the 2016 presidential election. Ron DeSantis, then the governor of Florida, told the Florida Family Council's GOP forum in 2018, "Getting into the bathroom wars . . . I don't think that's a good use of our time." Even then, presidential candidate Trump, riding the strongest swell of ultraconservative voter turnout in decades, criticized the North Carolina law during a televised town hall hosted by the *Today Show*. Considering that both these politicians would eventually build massive political capital by attacking the so-called woke agenda, the progression of NC HB 2 failure from 2016 to the drastic increase of similar bills in 2024 is remarkable.

From 2016 to 2024, in eight short years, the premise of NC HB 2, that transgender people could be legally disenfranchised, went from being an unmitigated disaster for Republicans to being their kingmaker issue. By 2024, Trump was championing this issue. Indeed, one of the most-aired political campaign attack ads by the Trump campaign in 2024 tied his opponent, Kamala Harris, to gender-affirming policies, while distancing Trump from them. As the commercial concluded, "Kamala is for they/them, but President Trump is for you." CNN called the ad one of the most influential of the campaign and reported that the Trump campaign spent over $10 million airing it in swing states alone. And on his first day in office, Trump signed an executive order designating that the United States recognized only two genders and sexes: male and female. Federal legislation would soon follow. By the winter of 2024, the first federal ban on bathroom usage came to Capitol Hill and was aimed at policing the gender of U.S. senators and representatives, as well as their staff and visitors, inside the restrooms within all federal buildings. Introduced by Republican Representative Nancy Mace from South Carolina, the bill coincided with the swearing in of the first out transgender representative to serve in the U.S. House of Representatives, Sarah McBride from Delaware. With its passage, McBride will be banned from using the proper bathroom at work.

How did we get here? It's not like transphobic legislation was suddenly eliminated from state assembly dockets after NC HB 2 failed, but the strategies around these types of bills shifted. As activist and journalist Erin Reed put it, "There was a good four-year period where anti-trans legislation sort of took the back seat. They kind of licked their wounds and they stepped back. And they started planning." NPR reports that after the dismantling of North

Carolina's house bill 2 in 2017, Terry Schilling, with the American Principles Project, a conservative think tank that led the charge to bring transgender bathroom bills back to the political forefront, met with former North Carolina Governor McCrory to reflect on the defeat. Schilling believed that transphobic legislation could still be a wedge issue Republicans could use to win over independent voters. For the next four years, Schilling and allies regrouped and rethought their strategy. The new tactics involved several important political adjustments. First, they focused on states with strong conservative bases and established leadership. States like North Carolina, that had flipped Democrat and Republican and back, both at the state and the national level, would be deemphasized, while states with Republican supermajorities would be targeted. In states where the Republican primary is often more contested than the general election, having a polarizing issue like an anti-trans agenda may function to distance some conservative candidates from the others. Reed asserted, "I don't think that [these bills] . . . win them elections. Now, where it may win them is in primaries." Hungry conservatives looking to break through the internal party chatter had found a useful soapbox.

Second, groups shopping these bills could limit the potential economic damage by starting in states that are immune to boycotts. Speaking to NPR, Schilling explained, "They really can't boycott Texas. It's just too big, and it's too much of an economic powerhouse." Indeed, if Texas were its own country, it would have the eighth-biggest economy in the world, with a gross domestic product larger than Canada's and Russia's. The second state that

9
Picking Our Ground

The bill passing through the legislature in Alabama tore me up, but it also burned off any romantic notions I had of the place and its people. I can always love Alabama the place, and I will certainly always love my friends and family in Alabama. But I had been naive about how well systems, like those entrenched in Alabama's state government, operate without and often in spite of sound argument or care. These systems are built to maintain themselves with the utmost efficiency by cleaving off whoever they can to hold on to the majority. Difference is the weapon of the system. If those in power can isolate and stigmatize a group of people, they draw the support they need from anyone not of that group who can rest easy in the notion that they are not *them*. These are not new or revolutionary ideas. They are the cornerstones of political polarization and the lifeblood of American political parties.

Even so, all of the anti-trans laws coming through the state and federal governments, including the one we were fighting in Alabama, reached the same bottleneck: the judicial system. Fighting the legislation in the courts felt different. The system is slower to come to a decision. Then there are appeals, which complicate both major rulings and individual motions within the trial itself.

Victories and defeats feel measured, incremental, and reversable. The process wears on you.

But there were also parts of the court battle that appealed to me. First, even when logic failed to persuade at the legislative level, surely it could be more impactful in a courtroom. And the application of that logic, building from point to point, precedent to precedent, fits so squarely into the way I process the world that I had hope that maybe, just maybe, this was the most promising position from which to fight this dragon. This could be our high ground. The state could not pretend the facts were with it, nor did it have the Constitution on its side. Perhaps logic could prevail here if nowhere else.

It should be said that I also put a lot of faith in judges. This is probably a holdover from my comfort with hegemony from years as a white man in the South, but it was reinforced by the numerous lawyers and judges I have met and gotten to know through the years. Many times, it was listening to the stories my father, my uncle, and all their lawyer friends would tell about their times in court. How even when they came out on the wrong side of a decision, they seemed to respect the process in which the decision was reached.

I was uncomfortably hopeful with the prospects of a trial. I still held out hope for this system as a constitutional bulwark for the rights of families like ours. But the trick to a lawsuit is that someone, or some group, has to step into the breach. You can't sue the state because it's unconstitutional on a grand scale; you have to step up and raise your hand and say, "Me, this law is unconstitutional to me." I was fine with that. I was ready to fight, and I was pissed that it had come this far. I was a professor of communication and a father of amazing daughters and an old debate coach. This was an arena in which I felt I could excel. I was raring to go. But it wasn't me they wanted—it was Kate. She was the one whose rights were being targeted, and she was scared of what this law meant to her. She wanted to be a part of the lawsuit, but I worried that she might not be ready.

When Asaf called to talk about how the NCLR was working with the other groups, like the ACLU and the Southern Poverty Law Center, to file their case, he said they had compared notes about their plaintiffs. It was an impressive roster, featuring physicians, families, and even preachers. Asaf and the others felt very good about the pool of plaintiffs and articulated where there was depth and where they had to be careful. As I understood it, the broadness of the bill affected a lot of people, so having representation from each affected group was vital. This lawsuit had that, because many families, doctors, and people who worked with trans children were ready to sue. That was the depth of the plaintiff pool. But care needed to be exercised to maximize the effectiveness of their arguments, because each plaintiff's experience was unique. As much as I wanted to testify, the lawsuit didn't need pissed-off fathers.

Specifically, they needed children who could talk about being trans and how they had benefited from gender-affirming care and what their lives would be like without it. When the NCLR interviewed Kate, and Rachel and I watched from the background, their questions focused on experiences she had not yet had. When the lawyers helped us construct declarations, Kate's youth did her no favors. The declaration is part of a filing that functions as plaintiff testimony before testimony in the trial can take place. As part of the NCLR filing, both Kate and I had declarations. I enjoyed creating mine. It was like constructing a debate argument with my real-life experiences and examples, concisely describing our family's progress, the joy Kate felt when supported, and the fear of what might return if Kate lost care.

Kate's experiences, though, came without my anxiety over her future. Kate was only thirteen years old at the time, and her contentment with being a young teenage girl was palpable. And she had not considered a world where she wasn't afforded that comfort and safety. Kate was a girl, that was concrete in her mind, so health care and support seemed inevitable. She could not fathom a world in which her doctors would not help her be who she was, and it showed in her declaration. As she talked with the lawyers, Rachel and I were just off camera, in the kitchen, and trying not to look like we were listening as intently as we were. The lawyers seemed to get what they wanted, promised to send documents our way, and signed off with upbeat goodbyes, but even at the time, we knew it wasn't great.

It was a strange space in which to find myself. Kate felt good, happy, and protected enough that she was not afraid, even in the face of stigmatization. Maybe that's because much of what the law was targeting was new for her. For one thing, Kate had just started puberty blockers not three months before the bill passed. Her time before had involved pediatricians, therapists, and endocrinologists who had affirmed her identity and treated her gender dysphoria with compassion, science, and care, so every doctor's visit involved her true name, and she was treated like the girl she is. She had only known

A big part of me wanted to believe her. She was thriving in this new place, and she did, in fact, have insightful opinions from years of living through all of these injustices. Did she get it? Did she understand the sacrifices and daily struggles? Had she been too insulated from it all, or were there scars and trauma there that I could not know or understand? Most likely, it was a combination that would take a lifetime to unpack. Where was she in that unpacking right now?

"So you feel like you are ready to do this?" I needed her to convince me. "Do you know what you want to tell people?"

She tossed her hair, which had fallen over her face as she stooped to pick up an acorn. She told me about the questions they had provided, and said, "They are easy to answer!"

"Easy how?" It hasn't taken me long to learn that what's easy for a fifteen-year-old to say is not always easy for a parent to hear.

She continued, "The Youth Outright folks want to ask about the new laws, like being blocked from joining sports, and I don't have that problem because I don't want to play sports."

"So your answer to is going to be 'I don't have to worry about that because I don't play sports'?"

"I mean, no?" That was exactly her plan.

"Kate, do you remember mini soccer?"

"Kind of."

"Do you remember swim team? How about karate?"

"I remember I didn't really like going to them."

"You should think about why you didn't like going to them. Because you loved swimming and you loving doing karate. But you are right, you did not like going. Why do you think that was?"

She sat quietly for a moment, either thinking or hoping the conversation was over. It's hard to tell with teenagers. "Do you remember roller derby?"

"Yeah, of course! That was great."

"But why? What made it better?" She could tell this was turning into a teaching moment, which she dreads, so I went for it before she could pull the plug. "Look, you've struggled through these issues your whole life. Maybe you weren't always traumatized by them, but even as a little kid, you altered your actions in public around being trans and the environments you found yourself in or were excluded from. If you want to do this panel, you have to think really hard about that, and you have to share that with other people. It won't be easy, if you're going deep. But it will be wonderful."

She promised she would, but it felt like she was only saying that to end the conversation.

I was a mess in the run-up to the panel. I kept thinking about the balance we'd had to strike for years, how we wanted to protect Kate from each and every obstruction and slight and how the stigmatization had gutted us. She was run out of schools and rejected from others, and even the best one we found came with assholes stopping by to scream at the trans kids on the playground. She was the one going to these schools, playing the sports, and getting the health care, while we tried to make each one a safe place for her. Kate being happy and healthy was the ultimate goal, so shouldn't I be happy that she seemed unfazed by years of navigating social norms, rules, and laws in a state that ultimately drove us out? No, not if she didn't understand what it took from her too. It's like when she was in first grade and the teacher refused to call her by her name. Kate internalized it, lived with it, and did not challenge it. I hated that for her then, but now I needed her to understand that just because she is happy, she doesn't have to let that teacher off the hook. What would first grade have been like if she had had a better teacher? It might have been the best year of her life instead of a daily struggle. Could she speak to that?

The event was well attended. Hosted at a downtown pottery studio, it quickly became standing-room only, despite seating for around forty. There were four students on the panel, with an adult moderator who led the discussion and asked the questions. The youth on the panel did an amazing job of talking about the laws. They discussed where they were in their lives and how they had been impacted in school, in sports, and in their search for health care. One high school student, clutching an opossum plush toy for comfort, described in vivid detail how their gender dysphoria made them feel all wrong and the crushing disappointment of knowing they would now have to try and live with it until they were eighteen. "I count down the hours," they said through tears. Another student described his efforts to remain stealthy at school, where the other high school boys were not kind and accepting. He avoided sports teams, PE classes, and the bathroom at school, finding ways to leave campus and keep busy in the afternoons with jobs to give him a ready excuse when classmates asked why he didn't play sports. The youngest student on the panel shared how they deal with deadnaming and the complications of school records and classroom behavior. These personal stories reflected the resilience of panelists, blending heart-wrenching experiences with clear-eyed optimism that they will fight through.

Kate took a notably different approach from everyone else from the word go. She made everyone laugh. She told stories about herself, her family, and her experiences in sports, schools, and health care, but she used the levity of her stories as a way to connect. Panelists, moderators, and audience members laughed out loud when Kate talked about her time in school and in sports and fighting the laws in Alabama. And, remarkably, the more they laughed, the more the audience seemed to lean in and listen.

And, of course, she poked fun at me. During the Q and A at the end, an audience member asked, "What do you wish adults knew about being transgender?" The other panelists talked about pronoun mistakes. When it was her turn, Kate opened with, "Being transgender is not easy, but you should all try having a debate coach for a father!" She had to wait a while for the laughter to die down before she told them all about me prepping for every encounter, including the panel, and challenging her to think more and prepare more. And then she said she was thankful for that support. With it, she could concentrate on finding the balance between being well informed and living her life joyfully. "I hope adults know that we get how hard this can be, but we don't need to be down on ourselves all the time. We just want to be kids too."

For the last fifteen years, I've been learning from Kate about how to be a father of a transgender kid in the rural South. I've made my share of mistakes. Some of my mistakes, like when I originally named her, were mistakes I could never see coming. Others, like putting her in sports again and again, were ones I probably should have seen coming. But the best part of my mistakes is that Kate relishes me

Appendix: For Readers' Reference

H-185.950 that an "established body of medical research" shows the medical effectiveness and necessity of "mental health care, hormone therapy, and sex reassignment surgery" in treating gender dysphoria. The AMA has resolved "that our American Medical Association support public and private health insurance coverage for treatment of gender identity disorder as recommended by the patient's physician."

Statements

- Clarification of Evidence-Based Gender-Affirming Care
  The AMA
    - recognizes that treatments for gender dysphoria and gender incongruence are medically necessary
    - will work with stakeholders to advocate for laws and policies that protect access to care, oppose laws and policies that impede the provision of care, support protections against liability for physicians and institutions who provide care and patients who seek it, and communicate about the importance of gender-affirming care
    - will advocate for coverage of gender-affirming care by public and private health insurer
  Date: 2023
- AMA Opposes Effort to Allow Discrimination Against Patients
  "This proposal marks the rare occasion in which a federal agency seeks to remove civil rights protections.

It legitimizes unequal treatment of patients by not only providers, health care organizations, and insurers, but also by the government itself—and it will harm patients. Such policy should not be permitted by the U.S. government, let alone proposed by it."

Date: June 12, 2020

- Statement on U.S. Supreme Court's Ruling on Title VII Cases

"As physicians, and as leaders in medicine, we believe that LGBTQ+ individuals must be protected from workplace discrimination in order to prevent negative health outcomes. The AMA supports everyone's access to quality, evidence-based health care regardless of gender or sexual orientation, and will continue to work diligently at the state and federal levels to expand access to medical services, reduce stigma in treating patients with unique needs and break down discriminatory barriers to care."

Date: June 15, 2020

- Transgender Prisoners Have Fundamental Right to Appropriate Care

"Prisoners have a fundamental right to access necessary and effective medical care, and that includes the full range of treatments for gender dysphoria. So argues a strongly worded friend-of-the-court brief filed by the AMA and other medical and mental health professional organizations."

Date: May 2019

Appendix: For Readers' Reference

- Health Insurance Coverage for Gender-Affirming Care of Transgender Patients

  "The AMA opposes any discrimination based on an individual's sex, sexual orientation or gender identity, opposes the denial of health insurance on the basis of sexual orientation or gender identity, and supports public and private health insurance coverage for treatment of gender dysphoria as recommended by the patient's physician."

  Date: 2019

- Removing Financial Barriers to Care for Transgender Patients H-185.950

  "Our AMA supports public and private health insurance coverage for treatment of gender dysphoria as recommended by the patient's physician."

  Date: 2016

About the Author

Sim Butler is a proud father, husband, and communication scholar from Alabama, where he is the director of the Alabama Debate Society and an associate professor in the Communication Studies Department at the University of Alabama, all of which converge around his family's fight for rights in the state they call home. Navigating the social, political, and cultural bedrock of the Deep South while advocating for health care, safe schools, and legal rights for his transgender daughter, Sim reflects on the journey to nurture, protect, and prepare his child for the world in which we live, a world we build with community, but also one plagued with dragons.

seemed to fit the bill: Florida. "They certainly can't boycott Florida," Schilling explained, "[It's] the home state of Walt Disney World." We saw this play out when Florida Governor DeSantis forwarded his "Don't Say Gay" agenda in 2021 and 2022, signing legislation that limited the mere mention of LGBTQ+ identity and topics in K–12 classrooms. Predictably, Disney pushed back, touching off a tit for tat between the enormous Orlando-based entertainment company and the governor's office. At one point, in April 2022, Disney threatened to pull $17 billion in planned investment in Walt Disney World. However, this was not some new, easily transferable business but a company so heavily invested and entrenched, both physically and economically, in the state of Florida that there was little the company could do to truly challenge the legislation. They could not pick up and move the forty-three square miles of theme parks and hotels and the infrastructure to support them. Moreover, individuals and groups lacked the gumption or the will to boycott the theme park, and Walt Disney World, which depends on visitors from all over the world, could not advocate for a boycott of the state and still keep the park viable. Instead of taking DeSantis to the mat, Disney and the state government settled their disputes.

Texas proved similarly fertile ground for anti-trans legislation. In 2021, Texas led the country in introducing the most anti-trans bills with sixteen different initiatives to limit the rights of transgender individuals. Most notably, the Texas legislature passed house bill 25, a law barring trans schoolchildren from playing sports. "The women's sports issue was the first thing that really took off," said Schilling, "because it had that magic formula of having an incredible amount of public support amongst the American people, but also politicians were willing to run on it and campaign on it." Much of public opinion around these bills, as I've discussed, comes down to optics: framing the issue with the visual of a masculine-looking trans woman dominating the competition against smaller girls stirs powerful feelings of unfairness and potential injury. Women's sports are having some of their best years since Title IX was adopted, but the fearmongering of sneaky transgender women athletes bullying cisgender women and dominating competition threatens more than just the business of women's sports, it taps into what many believe is the sanctity of the events.

With the passage of HB 25 in Texas, other states quickly followed with similar bills. Finally, conservatives had the anti-trans wedge issue they could translate from Republican primaries to general elections. To make the issue salient, Americans needed to believe that there were a lot of trans athletes out there hoping to compete. Despite widespread media coverage of a couple of cases, the actual number of transgender athletes is miniscule. As the head of the NCAA, Charlie Baker told the U.S. Senate in December 2024 there were fewer than ten athletes he knew to be transgender participating in college athletics. As a point of reference, that's out of a total of the approximately 510,000 student athletes under NCAA jurisdiction, or less than 0.002 percent. But campaigning on the fear of a transgender takeover was far more potent than reporting factual numbers. When West Virginia governor (soon to be senator) Jim Justice signed the law that banned transgender youth from sports

Beyond Alabama

in his state, he was asked if he could point to a specific example of a transgender athlete in the state who was attempting to compete. "No, I can't really tell you one" was his response. And he didn't need to, because even if no example existed, the narrative resonated. By 2024, half the states in America had laws banning transgender children from youth sports.

As Schilling prophesized, anti-trans sports bills opened the door for the flood of anti-trans legislation. If legislators can claim to be protecting young women from trans invaders on the field, those same fearmongering tactics link easily to places like locker rooms, bathrooms, and classrooms. Because once the public accepts that transgender folks are the dangerous aggressors in a certain space, it becomes much easier to ban them from other spaces. And through vilifying transgender people, the mere presence of LGBTQ+ folks becomes a trigger for legislation, such as limiting access to health care for trans youth and banning the discussion of LGBTQ+ issues and identity in schools. Arizona and Tennessee forwarded legislation to ban drag shows. Idaho took a swing at marriage equality. South Carolina attempted to legislate the word *transgender* out of existence.

The ACLU counted thirty-five bills in 2023 alone targeting health care access for transgender people, fifty-eight bills aimed at LGBTQ+ rights in schools and educational settings, nineteen bills focused on the freedom of speech and expression for LGBTQ+ people, four bills written to limit the right to accurate identity documents for transgender people, seven bills seeking to weaken existing civil rights laws, and several more that targeted LGBTQ+

rights generally. The sheer quantity of legislation targeting transgender folks and the greater queer community was staggering, particularly when you consider how small this community is. YouGov published the results of polling Americans in March 2022 about the ubiquity of transgender persons in America, and respondents vastly overestimated the number of transgender folks, guessing that it was one in five, or 20 percent of Americans. But the number is closer to 0.6 percent of Americans.

There are at least two important takeaways from these numbers. First, it makes for a lopsided political battle. Because Americans, for one reason or another, think transgender individuals are more common than they are, dangerous and stigmatizing myths about LQBTQ+ people recruiting and grooming youth, parents pressuring their children to change their gender, and transgender students creating unsafe environments at schools and in sports have more impact than they might otherwise. This gives legislators the ability to overemphasize the magnitude of transgender inclusion without fear of political reprisal, as transgender voters make up such a tiny population. Thus, these bills will continue to be introduced and moved through state legislatures until allies step up to provide the type of backlash NC HB2 faced in 2016.

The second important takeaway is scope: State legislators are considering over six hundred bills a year legislating the lives of 0.6 percent of the population. Take, for example, the bans on gender-affirming care. In order to pass such laws, common tactics are to inflate and overemphasize the rate at which gender-affirming care is sought, creating the impetus for action to protect the (exaggerated) number of children seeking this care and leading twenty-six states, more than half the country, to ban the practice. When researchers from the Harvard School of Public Health surveyed the medical records of over 5 million private medical insurance users, only 0.1 percent of patients asked for gender-affirming care. The staggeringly disproportionate amount of scrutiny and stigmatization has real-world consequences for people.

Nex Benedict was a sixteen-year-old nonbinary student in Oklahoma who died from an apparent suicide the day after being beaten unconscious in their school's bathroom. Nex enjoyed being in nature, watching the television show *The Walking Dead*, and playing *Minecraft*. The attack on Nex and their best friend went unreported by the school, despite witnesses recounting that a group attacked Nex, repeatedly slamming their head against the ground until they lost consciousness. Why the attack went unreported by the school is an unanswered question, but it follows a clear pattern. Oklahoma, where Nex attended school, bans trans people from using bathrooms and facilities that align with their gender identity in K–12 schools. States that pass these laws put queer students at risk, because they encourage the invasive practice of policing bodies, which often becomes an excuse for state and vigilante violence.

Attacks like the one on Nex are a regular occurrence for transgender, nonbinary, and queer-identifying students. Data from the Human Rights Council and the University of Connecticut's 2023 LGBTQ+ Youth Report illustrate the alarming regularity with which students are harassed, bullied, and attacked while attempting to use the bathroom at school. Of trans and gender-expansive youth surveyed, 62.6 percent had been teased or bullied at school at least once in the prior year, and the majority of them were teased specifically for their LGBTQ+ identity. Additionally, 20 percent of the children surveyed had been hit or pushed or had experienced other forms of physical violence at school in just the thirty days prior to the survey. Understandably, 53.9 percent of trans and gender-expansive youth feel unsafe in at least one school setting, with a third, 32.8 percent, reporting that they specifically felt unsafe in school restrooms, and nearly half, 49.3 percent, reporting that they felt unsafe in school locker rooms. And before you argue that high school is tough for everyone, take a moment and apply these numbers to any other student group. If 20 percent of the marching band was physically assaulted every month, schools would certainly take steps to reduce that violence. Yet the opposite is true in the case of LGBTQ+ students in schools, and particularly in bathrooms. They are made out to be the perpetrators of violence, and so little to no protection is afforded them by the authorities passing these laws. Framed as the villains by those in power and attacked by their peers, it's no wonder that 82 percent of transgender individuals have considered killing themselves and 40 percent have attempted suicide.

Ultimately, the violence encouraged by the laws vilifying an already vulnerable and targeted group has begot even more draconian policies. In 2022, Texas began enforcing a directive from Republican Governor Greg Abbott to investigate the guardians of trans youth as serial child abusers. The state's family policing agency, the Texas Department of Family Protective Services (DFPS), continues to target the families of transgender youth in abuse investigations, despite several court challenges and a mass exodus of employees. Under Abbott's directive, transgender students as young as eighth grade are being pulled from their classrooms to answer questions by authorities about their family's support of their identity. Teachers use social media to collect evidence that a student might be trans and report their findings to DFPS. And many queer youth now find themselves trapped in the custody of the state, where they don't feel safe to be themselves. And the actions of Abbott and the DFPS victimize an already vulnerable population. The Trevor Project reports that homelessness and housing instability are extremely high among transgender (39 percent) and nonbinary (35 percent) youth, particularly because queer youth often face rejection and expulsion from their families. In one survey, 40 percent of respondents reported being kicked out or abandoned because of their LGBTQ+ identity, while 55 percent reported running away from home because of mistreatment or fear of mistreatment because of their LGBTQ+ identity. Texas has effectively taken a group with drastically high rates of abandonment and declared that the homes that are supportive and accepting of them shall be considered abusive. Not only does it give cover to any parent considering rejecting their child for who they are or for who they love but it also effectively declares that transgender youth can have no home whatsoever.

If the Texas legislature teaches us anything, it's that these laws can, and will, continue to get worse. In 2025, Texas floated a law that made identifying yourself as transgender a felony.

Law by law, bill by bill, decision by decision, states across America have publicly declared that transgender children are dangerous, unlovable, and not worth protecting. The lengths to which legislative bodies have gone to make it clear that violence toward transgender children is acceptable emboldens citizens to enact violence of their own. It's no surprise that in 2021, the year anti-trans legislation increased across the country by 253 percent, there were at least fifty-seven transgender and gender nonconforming people murdered, the largest number of fatal trans violence incidents recorded in a single year since the Human Rights Council began tracking this violence in 2013.

Just as the number of anti-trans bills increased in 2022, the murders of transgender youth increased. Ariyanna Mitchell was a junior in high school when she was shot at a party in April 2022. According to reports, Ariyanna was asked if she was trans, and when she answered in the affirmative, she was shot and killed. Ariyanna was a member of the Triple E Dance Academy. Her parents recounted, "She was truly unique, funny, and loved by everyone. There was never a dull moment when Ariyanna was around." She was seventeen years old.

Pauly Likens, a transgender girl from Pennsylvania, was tracked down on social media before being murdered and dismembered in July 2024. Her obituary tells us that Pauly was "a selfless person never missing a chance to help others and give what she could" and "lit up every room she entered, always making people smile and passing around her contagious laughter." She was fourteen years old.

The Trans Day of Remembrance was founded in 1999 by transgender advocate Gwendolyn Ann Smith as a vigil to honor the memory of Rita Hester, a transgender woman who was killed the year before. Each November, the day marks an opportunity to grieve and honor the transgender community members struck down by violence. In the words of the founder,

> [The] Transgender Day of Remembrance seeks to highlight the losses we face due to anti-transgender bigotry and violence. I am no stranger to the need to fight for our rights, and the right to simply exist is first and foremost. With so many seeking to erase transgender people—sometimes in the most brutal ways possible—it is vitally important that those we lose are remembered, and that we continue to fight for justice.

When I look at pictures of Nex, Ariyanna, and Pauly, I see my daughter Kate. It doesn't matter if the kids in those pictures had straight hair or braids, liked music or soccer, wanted to be lawyers or artists when they grew up. I see my daughter because each was a young person who was attacked simply for being trans or nonbinary. I encourage everyone to go and read their obituaries. I understand if anyone needs to skip them, because some of you may know this violence and loss all too well. For those of you who do read them, I'll be surprised if you don't think of children in your own lives, because the joyful innocence of being a kid saturates their parents' descriptions. If you have kids, know kids, and love kids, these obituaries will be a hard read, because you'll recognize their parents' love through the lens of your own love. I feel that too, but I have another reason why I tear up. When I read their obituaries, the similarities crush my heart, because I have to consider what I might have to include in Kate's someday.

And if you get to the end of this chapter and you feel the enormity of the struggle that these kids face all over our country and you ask, What can I do?, I'll tell you that you already know. If you can love any kids, then love these kids too, just the way they are. In the face of overwhelming stigmatization and policing, these kids need your love. Do your best to show it to them before their parents have to memorialize them.

gender-affirming health care ever since she had begun socially transitioning at age six. She could not really speak to life before transitioning because not only had it happened long ago in that fuzzy space of early childhood but in her mind it was done, and she had moved on. For Kate, she looked like a girl, she had a girl's name, and she was treated like a girl. In every community we placed her in, supporting her gender journey was a make or break for our family: Kate is a girl.

Now, at the very cusp of puberty, she had no concept of what she was avoiding. Nor could she speak to the advantages of receiving medical intervention or how detrimental it would be to have a lack of the proper health care she had just began to use because she had never been forced to be without it. She didn't have the pain of the distress that would come from pronounced facial hair, a deeper voice, and a masculine build, nor did she yet have any fear of those things. Those were unthinkable horrors, yes, but Kate thinks and feels in the present, and worried little about the future. If she had had to live those developments, even temporarily, she would have been terrified. But that had not been her reality, and, thus, would not be her future. In her mind, no matter what, she was still going to be Kate, the girl whose gender no one would question. That makes for a proud parent, to be sure, because it feels like we did our job as parents. Our child was happy and healthy, with no fear of the future despite its dangers. At the same time, since Kate could not speak to what she had not experienced yet, it made for a pretty weak declaration.

It's also important to remember that a declaration is carefully crafted by your lawyers, who know what questions to ask to maximize the answer's potential effectiveness. The declaration is only a taste of what is to come: a plaintiff who is willing to testify.

The witness stand is a lonely place, even in the best of situations. Alone, elevated for clear sight lines, your only tool is your voice, and it must be used precisely. Even as I thought of being in that space myself, I could feel my nerves.

I asked Asaf, "How do you feel about the children you have as plaintiffs?"

"Well, pretty good." He then described the other families and children. Most were older teens who had experience with hormone therapy beyond only blockers. They were articulate, and their stories were compelling.

"Do you think they will all have to testify?"

"It's hard to say," Asaf cleared his throat. "We will prepare the case with the plan to have everyone ready to testify. In a case like this, we are trying to articulate the undue harm to individuals as much as the general unconstitutional nature of the law, so the testimony is really important." There is a pregnant pause. "Are you worried about Kate testifying?"

"Of course! I mean, aren't you?"

"Well, probably not in the same ways you are." Asaf, bless his heart, was still trying to be gentle with us. "I'm sure you're worried about Kate's anonymity, which we can request in the filings but may not be upheld, and, even if it was, her testimony in court would run counter to her being incognito." Another pause. I appreciated what he was doing, giving us the outs we might hadn't thought of yet. "And I know you've considered the pressure of testifying in court. I doubt the lawyers from the state would be rude or overly harsh, but it's a lot to ask a thirteen-year-old to do, especially considering the nature of their questions. Even gentle questions will need to probe how Kate understands her gender, her sex, and her body."

He didn't need to say it. We knew it already. These were Kate's most private and dear ideas. They were the world on which her mental well-being rested. You take that child and you subject them to a skilled, prepared adult, whose primary job is to discredit the child's most dear sense of self. What were the consequences of cross-examination?

Then an even darker thought bloomed. What if they lost the case, and she blamed herself? She could trace the stigmatization and disenfranchisement of people she knew and cared about, of herself, to a moment she barely could control but might feel totally responsible for. We would be placing her in an almost impossible position with the potential for lifelong consequences. Can a thirteen-year-old even conceive what that burden might be?

"Tell me this," I said, "how confident would you feel putting Kate on the stand?"

"Well, if Kate were the only teen we had, I'd feel great about what she could contribute. From our perspective, we need to maximize the testimony at our disposal to make our arguments. Since Kate's experience is limited to only just starting puberty blockers, and y'all have done a fine job of finding her appropriate care as she socially transitioned, we'd have to use other testimony to illustrate the true harms of the lack of gender-affirming care."

"Okay, so Kate's testimony doesn't paint the entire picture needed. Do you have other plaintiffs whose testimony is more comprehensive?

"Absolutely."

"And would you feel just as good moving forward without Kate?"

"Yes. Kate's testimony was vital before, but not at this time. Her story is beautiful and important, but it is not unique among our plaintiffs."

And there it was. Kate did not have to testify for the case to be strong. We didn't have to put her in a courtroom, in front of a judge and opposition lawyers who might very well try to tear down the very essence of who she was. I was utterly relieved. But I also felt I could not abandon the others, who would so bravely face the courtroom.

"Asaf, you are our lawyer. What would you recommend?" I did not know what to do; I was torn. I wanted my daughter to be able to face down this dragon, but I did not want her to have to. I did not think she was ready, and it was a reflection on me, not on her. I had not done enough quickly enough to prepare her, and for that I felt shame. Was I failing her, our family, and all the other families who needed this battle won?

"It's your decision," he said. "The case is strong and can move ahead without you. But there is no guarantee that we win, and any decision will ultimately take years. And even if we do, you'll still have to be living in ambiguity surrounding health care, limits on rights, and clear hostility."

And then he added: "If it were me, I would get my family out of Alabama." It was as clear a recommendation as could have been possibly made. We thanked him and promised to contact him again soon, and with that, we wrapped up the call.

Rachel and I needed to process what we were feeling. For years,

Picking Our Ground

we had talked about our rip cord. When does our life here become untenable? At what point do you stop this free fall, pull the cord, and parachute to safety? At first it was an intellectual exercise, attempting to weigh our blessings—like good friends, careers, and community—against an existential, nearly unquantifiable threat. As it happened, it became a regular tallying. As the threats became more tangible, the rip cord became more real. We made Excel spreadsheets of "If this, then what?" If the state passes the law, what's next? How quickly do we have to move and where do we go? And every calculation came with a cost. Sell the house now or later, when the market is better? Shutter the business or wait and try to sell it? What about my career? Do I move with the family or hang back for my job? How far do we go? Far enough to be safer but close enough that it feels a little like home? Where is that, exactly? Is it Virginia, California, or New Zealand? We did not have the answers, only the questions. But in talking to Asaf, it felt like this was our rip cord moment. Stay longer, and we'd put Kate in more risk than we were willing to, whether she testified or not.

In May 2023, the family left Alabama and regrouped. We stayed in the South, but we picked a more purple state, meaning it was not dominated by politicians trying to outflank one another to the right. We sought refuge among friends and family and found some semblance of peace. To feel that for the first time in years, that finally we were not under attack, was a salve for my soul. I had not understood what the battle was doing to me until I had some respite from it. Even with this newfound peace, it was impossible not to look back over our shoulders, especially since I was constantly living between my work in Alabama and my family living elsewhere.

We left others to cover our retreat, and I will always be thankful to those who stayed to fight. We've continued to follow the court battle closely. With plaintiffs spread all over the state, there was some speculation as to where the case would land. It settled in Judge Liles Burke's court in Limestone County. Burke, a Trump appointment to the bench, was ideologically much more conservative than many advocates had hoped for. Nevertheless, preliminary hearings seemed to go our way. After hearing testimony and weighing arguments, Burke granted the plaintiffs a preliminary injunction, temporarily halting the ability of the state to enforce the law until a full trial could take place. In his decision, Burke followed the same logic I had always hoped would prevail: that the leading medical professional associations unanimously agree that gender-affirming care is best for the patients and that families of transgender children and overwhelmingly support access to gender-affirming care. Judge Burke also noted that the state failed to produce a single witness, expert or otherwise, from the state of Alabama to speak in favor of the law. Most importantly, he wrote that the law was most likely unconstitutional, as the U.S Supreme Court has regularly ruled that parents have a fundamental right to direct the medical care of their children and that discrimination based on gender nonconformity equates to sex discrimination. As I have argued, regardless of ideological leanings, and even from a staunchly conservative one, the law was probably unconstitutional.

We celebrated this win knowing it might not last. Sure enough, the state appealed the injunction and had it overturned, thus paving the way for the state to continue enforcing the law and making doctors and parents felons. Even though Judge Burke outlined the flaws in the state's case, a trial begins the arguments anew. As more states followed with their own transphobic legislation, the cases against those state governments from medical professionals, advocates, and families piled up. Precedent was being set, appealed, and set again, with lawyers, advocacy groups, and judges carefully watching. So even if Judge Burke came to the conclusions we hoped he would, higher courts could first rule totally differently, codifying a precedent for everyone else.

This is exactly what happened in the summer of 2025. In the winter of 2024, the Supreme Court heard arguments on *United States v. Skrmetti*, in which families seeking gender-affirming health care in Tennessee challenged the constitutionality of the laws preventing care. For the first time ever, an openly transgender lawyer, Chase Strangio, made arguments in front of America's highest court. Considering the court currently has what many consider to be six conservative judges and only three liberal-leaning judges, Strangio and colleagues had an uphill battle. Predictably, the court voted along ideological lines and against the families and advocates seeking gender-affirming care protections. The case not only became legal precedent around the country, setting the stage for federal and state recourse against health care systems across the United States, the arguments used to justify the decision highlighted the tactics used to perpetuate the injustice.

As before, selective reading of the research was used to prop up social misgivings around the issue. Supreme Court Justice Alito specifically pushed back on the idea that gender-affirming care prevented suicide, questioning whether studies that show increased depression, anxiety, and suicidality among transgender youth who lacked access to gender-affirming care were enough to argue that gender-affirming care actually prevented suicide. Strangio conceded that they did not. The studies clearly showed a relationship between a lack of care and a toxic brew of feelings that can lead to suicide, but they could not definitively prove that care prevented suicide.

Of course, the line of questioning from Alito, like many of the questions around gender identity, is a trick. It cherry-picks the results, the data, and methodologies in order to discredit the findings. Think about this: How could someone prove that gender-affirming care prevents suicide? The most reasonable way to do this, as researchers, advocates, parents, and Strangio argued, is to ask the kids who received the care. Only they could know if they wanted to live or die. By asking kids who received gender-affirming care what they think would have happened if they hadn't received care, researchers captured a glimpse into what could motivate someone to commit suicide. Over and over again, the responses were the same, as articulated in the Alabama state house committee meeting I attended. A trans youth that day told that committee of legislators that without gender-affirming medical care, "I would not be here."

That said, to Judge Alito's point, the research does not create a causal link, as it relies on personal speculation. Let me put it this way: Even if a child were to tell researchers that they feel strongly that they would have killed themselves without care, it doesn't prove that they actually would have, only that they report that they think they would have. But what study could prove this? The study that Alito was asking for, the only one that matters to him in this context, cannot exist. It would need a medium to answer, because the only way to definitively prove that gender-affirming care prevents suicide is to study the motivations of the ones who committed suicide. That is, you'd have to ask the dead kids.

The Supreme Court's decision will have long-lasting and far-reaching ramifications on health care access and civil rights. How far the disenfranchisement stretches and how long it lasts remains to be seen. I spend a lot of time speculating about the outcomes, and the old ripcord feelings come back. When do we pull the cord and escape and how far do we have to go? It's easy for me to sink into these thoughts, and, when I do, I feel helpless, confused, and frustrated.

What pulls me away from these feelings is when the work is right in front of my eyes. When I am actively striving to build a home for my family, it's easier to feel that the love we give makes a difference. That's because I get to watch my kids grow up, and the joy it brings me keeps me afloat. After years of trying to make it work, of settling, and of struggling, we moved the family, and we landed in a little spot with just a touch of queer visibility, a lot of community, and it still felt like home. Not long after we moved in, we went down to the closest brewery for dinner. By a stroke of luck, it was hosting an event called Queers and Beers, an annual celebration of LGBTQ+ resilience, with discount draft beer and a handful of booths set up between the brewery and the dog park. My children saw pride flags in classrooms at school, read welcome signs that felt welcoming, and found organizations that work to support queer youth by holding get-togethers. It was so wonderfully casual, like it was part of the fabric of the place, that my kids felt settled very quickly.

In this place, Kate continues to blossom. When the local chapter of Youth Outright hosted a Youth Speaks event in early 2024, Kate was asked to be one of the panelists. I was suddenly and unexpectantly nervous. Unlike the other Youth Outright events she attends, where they play *Dungeons & Dragons*, offer educational support, or just hang out, this was billed as a young person's protest of the laws our new state was pushing through the legislature. Many were the same laws we had seen before: banning trans kids from sports and bathrooms and prohibiting access to gender-affirming health care. Organized so adults could ask the children how these laws affect them, the event gave a handful of transgender, nonbinary, and/or gender-diverse high school students an opportunity to talk about their own experiences, leading to discussions of gender dysphoria, bullying at school, and depression and anxiety.

I have experience with such panels; I have spoken to groups for years about our family's trials, missteps, and joys. But here I was, putting Kate on the stand in my place, the exact thing we had decided against not long ago. Now fifteen, was she ready? She thought she was, but Rachel and I weren't so sure. While walking our dog one morning, I tried to voice these concerns with Kate. I told her she had to prepare for this panel if she wanted to do it.

"Prepare?" She shot me a side-eyed look that only teenagers can master and downshifted into a comforting kindergarten tone. "Daddy, I'm totally prepared."

having to admit to them every now and then. And as she gets older, she's getting better at pointing out more and more of them. As I sat in the audience of the event that day, she called out two mistakes in one fell swoop. The first was worrying that she wasn't ready to talk about herself. Kate blossomed that day, which I was hopeful she could do, so I was thrilled to have gotten that one wrong.

But the second mistake she recognized took me aback. Kate showed me that the dragon we had been fighting for years in Alabama wasn't her dragon, it was mine. It was Rachel and I who stayed up at night planning and who toiled every day to keep that dragon at bay. Once Kate came out, we created such a shield for her that she grew into a happy, healthy kid. She didn't have to dip into her reserves to fight our dragon, so she was stronger and prepared, ready for the next one that came along.

Epilogue

Upon taking office in January 2025, President Donald Trump immediately signed a slew of executive orders curtailing the rights, freedoms, and protections of transgender and nonbinary folks in the United States. Meanwhile, conservatives in the U.S. Congress began drafting and debating many of the same laws passed at the state level since 2021. Many of these executive and legislative actions had immediate and chilling effects on the lives of transgender people, their families, and allies of the LGBTQ+ community. The Department of State froze passport applications for transgender citizens, medical care was stripped from families of military personnel and their families, and threats to cut funding for hospitals paralyzed gender clinics across the nation. Based on numerous news reports and the conversations I'm having with allies and families of transgender folks across the nation, so many people are having the same rip cord conversations my family had back in the early 2020s. Unfortunately, these steps were not unexpected. They follow a familiar playbook, and they bring up the same questions for families like ours: What do we do now? Where do we go? And I doubt transgender folks are the only ones having these hard conversations, as other minority groups are also being singled out by this administration.

Epilogue

On the wall of the U.S. Holocaust Memorial Museum in Washington, DC, there is permanent display of a quote from the German theologian Martin Niemöller. It says,

> *First they came for the socialists, and I did not speak out—because I was not a socialist.*
> *Then they came for the trade unionists, and I did not speak out—because I was not a trade unionist.*
> *Then they came for the Jews, and I did not speak out—because I was not a Jew.*
> *Then they came for me—and there was no one left to speak for me.*

Interestingly, Niemöller had enthusiastically welcomed the Nazi regime in 1933. He identified with many of the far-right ideologies expounded by the Nazi Party, including hypernationalism, anticommunism, and anti-Semitism. However, as a Lutheran pastor, he became disillusioned with the Nazi Party when they began interfering with the church. On July 1, 1937, the Gestapo arrested Niemöller and imprisoned him for the next eight years. Niemöller was not freed until May 1945, when the Allies defeated Nazi Germany and liberated him and other concentration camp prisoners.

Touring the world after his release, Niemöller spoke on his naivete and shame over his role within a culture that systematically stigmatized, dehumanized, and stripped the rights of millions. His quote, often used in his speeches, speaks to our natural inclination to other-ize for political or social gain as well as to our hesitancy to speak up for those different from ourselves, even when we recognize injustice.

Herein lie both our greatest strength and most dangerous weakness as democratic citizens. When we construct our laws, our bills of rights, our constitutions to protect those other than ourselves, we build a pluralistic community that grows stronger together. Using our own beliefs and experiences as common ground, we can come together around what we all agree on. When we are united, we are the most powerful organization the world knows.

But when we define ourselves and others through our differences, we start down a dangerous path that elevates some over others, often simply for the sake of winning. Steve Bannon, a chief strategist and confidant in President Trump's first administration, acknowledged as much when he told *The American Prospect*'s Bob Kuttner, "The longer they talk about identity politics, I got 'em. I want them to talk about racism every day. If the left is focused on race and identity.... We can crush the Democrats." When someone spots racism and calls it out, it's a natural but dangerous assumption for someone else to conclude *I'm not the problem, because I'm not racist.* When we remove ourselves from struggles others face for rights, life, and liberty, we weaken the republic that is so precariously balanced on an economy of goodwill and respect for others. In the words of Dr. Martin Luther King Jr., "Injustice anywhere is a threat to justice everywhere."

At the end of the day, the anti-trans legislation, court battles, and cultural backsliding will most likely continue. There will be progress and regression, as is the natural flow of justice. It feels like

Epilogue

I could be writing this book forever if I waited for the end of this battle and likely never really find a conclusion, because Kate will always face an uphill battle for acceptance. And sometimes, I'm not sure that should even be the goal, because there will always be the tendency to out-American others by vilifying the different. Maybe the goal is less about winning this particular battle and, instead, about learning how best to apply the important lessons of our struggle for rights and dignity. I believe that success is better measured by how I grow in my compassion for others and in my tenacity to defeat injustices I have not experienced myself. But on a grander scale, those goals are only achieved when we work together; so I urge you to fight with us. Stay vigilant against injustice, particularly injustice toward the vulnerable, the scared, and the different, and I promise to do the same. Someday, even if you are not there yet, you may find yourself ousted socially, culturally, or politically for who you love, how you pray, or how you look. And if I'm still around, I'll stand beside you.

Acknowledgments

This book would not have been possible without a considerable amount of support for myself, my family, and this project. First, thank you to all my friends who took the time to read, listen, reminisce, and workshop both the concept of this manuscript and drafts of the chapters. Your patience, insight, and memories were invaluable. I'm sure you'll see your influence throughout, and I hope it reminds you how much you mean to us.

Second, I want to thank all the professionals who have supported and continue to support my family as we navigate our lives, including the doctors, lawyers, teachers, editors, counselors, pastors, book agent, and community advocacy groups and activists. Many of you go unnamed in these pages, but your impact on our lives has been immense. We had too many wonderful interactions of when the professionals did more than their job required to care for us to recount in the book, and I am eternally grateful.

Next, I want to thank my family, both blood and chosen, who fought tooth and nail alongside us to preserve a home for us and for families like ours. Even when we struggled the most, we always felt your love, and we could never have come to create a space as safe and wonderful as we have now without you.

Acknowledgments

Finally, I want to acknowledge the patience, resiliency, and tenacity of my wife and my children through this process. Not only am I proud of how you have fought these dragons with me, your grace and support in having me recount these struggles in print has felt unwavering. I feel honored to tell our story.

Appendix: For Readers' Reference

Below you will find the published stance from both the World Medical Association and the American Medical Association, the largest international and national medical associations of doctors, supporting gender-affirming care. I pulled these from the Advocates of Trans Equality's website (https://transhealthproject.org/resources/medical-organization-statements), where you can find the individual statements in support of gender-affirming care for the many leading health organizations mentioned in chapter 6.

World Medical Association

WMA is an international organization representing physicians. It was created to ensure the independence of physicians and to work for the highest possible standards of ethical behavior and care by physicians, at all times. Membership consists of 114 national medical associations.

Statements on Transgender People

The WMA recommends, among other things, the following principles:

Appendix: For Readers' Reference

1. "The WMA emphasises that everyone has the right to determine one's own gender and recognises the diversity of possibilities in this respect. The WMA calls for physicians to uphold each individual's right to self-identification with regards to gender.
2. The WMA asserts that gender incongruence is not in itself a mental disorder; however, it can lead to discomfort or distress, which is referred to as gender dysphoria (DSM-5).
3. The WMA affirms that, in general, any health-related procedure or treatment related to an individual's transgender status, e.g., surgical interventions, hormone therapy or psychotherapy, requires the freely given informed and explicit consent of the patient.
4. The WMA urges that every effort be made to make individualised, multi-professional, interdisciplinary and affordable transgender healthcare (including speech therapy, hormonal treatment, surgical interventions and mental healthcare) available to all people who experience gender incongruence in order to reduce or to prevent pronounced gender dysphoria."

Date: October 2015

American Medical Association

The American Medical Association, the largest association of physicians and medical students in the United States, articulates in